ICS Publications
2131 Lincoln Road, NE
Washington, DC 20002-1199

www.icspublications.org

Typeset and produced in the United States of America

Library of Congress Cataloging in Publication Data

Deeney, Aloysius, 1948-
Welcome to the Secular Order of Discalced Carmelites / by Aloysius Deeney.
p. cm.
ISBN 978-0-935216-75-2
1. Secular Order of Discalced Carmelites. 2. Spiritual life--Catholic Church.
I. Title.
BX3251.D44 2009
255'.971--dc22
2009019950

Contents

Introduction

This book is a collection of the conferences Fr. Aloysius Deeney presented to the Secular Order of Discalced Carmelite (OCDS) members on various occasions. Immediate interest in his talks was evident when the transcriptions of his conferences began to appear on numerous Carmelite Web sites worldwide. Encouraged by the interest of the OCDS communities and the importance of his talks for their formation programs in particular, the talks were compiled into four different booklets for printing and distribution. The interest in the booklets was enormous, and they were reprinted numerous times. As more and more OCDS communities tell the success stories of their formation programs with the help of these booklets, we decided to get the necessary assistance from ICS Publications for publication and distribution. The result is the book in your hand: *Welcome to the Secular Order of Discalced Carmelites*.

This book includes eight talks and a question-and-answer session, titled "Notes of Clarification." Our general observation is that those who come to Carmel show a great deal of interest in Carmelite spirituality and the writings of our Carmelite saints. As newcomers, they soon learn the process of becoming a Secular Carmelite in a community setting (Aspirant, Candidate) and their eventual reception into the membership of the Secular branch of the Discalced Carmelite Order as professed members. The newcomer begins to realize the importance of learning and assimilating the spirit of the teachers of Carmel within the context of a community setting.

Fr. Deeney brings to our attention the need for creating an atmosphere for individuals to learn and incorporate the spirit of Carmel into their daily lives. What he observes in the OCDS communities is the lack of an adequate formation program. A program of formation, as he explains, is not a program of information, that is, only what to teach in this period and what books to use in this period, etc. Instead, a program of formation is information on "how do we train people, how do we educate people, how do we inform people so that they make progress in the stages of formation. . . ." Hence, his talks are not about spirituality only but also cover topics involving governance, organization, and formation in the Secular Order of Discalced Carmelites.

Realizing the importance of nurturing strong and mature communities, Fr. Deeney's first major talk deals directly with the criteria for admitting prospective members to the Order. How many of us have grappled with the question of discernment and vocation to Carmel? Who is called to be a Secular Carmelite? How do you distinguish between those called and those who are not called? Fr. Deeney's most practical and insightful talks help one to understand the vocation to Carmel.

Another important aspect of his talks is about raising awareness in the Order for new Constitutions for the Secular Carmelites. At the OCDS International Congress in 2000, Fr. Deeney made the following proposal:

> My first point for review is the use of the title "Rule." In the history of spirituality, the word Rule has been reserved for the most part to designate the original inspiration of the great spiritual traditions of religious orders in the Church. Generally, the Rules are the Rule of Saint Benedict, the Rule of Saint Francis, the Rule of Saint Augustine, and the Rule of Saint Albert in the Western Church and the Rule of Saint Basil in the Eastern Church. These rules are approved by the Church. The entire family of Carmel has only one

> Rule, that of Saint Albert. By the phrase "the entire family of Carmel," I mean the friars, nuns affiliated and aggregated institutes, both religious and secular of both branches of the Order. In addition to the Rule of Saint Albert, and for the purposes of clarification and application, we all have Constitutions and/or Norms that accompany the Rule. The only group of Carmelites that has another "rule" is the Secular Order. I would like to propose that the Secular Order join the rest of the Order in preserving the word Rule for the Rule of Saint Albert and, in place of the word Rule, designate the proper legislation of the Secular Order as Norms for Carmelite Seculars. I think that it would help us all to unite together under the one Rule.

Fr. Deeney's proposal that the Secular Order join the rest of the Order in preserving the word "Rule" for the Rule of Saint Albert was an important moment in the history of the Secular Order. Not too long after his proposed new vision for the Secular Order, the Vatican, on June 16, 2003, approved the new OCDS constitutions: "May the new text of the Constitutions of the Secular Order of the Discalced Carmelites be a really effective means, so that its members can reinvigorate more and more their baptismal consecration in the concrete situations of family, social, civilian, and ecclesial life."

With the introduction of the new Constitutions, the Secular Order gained a new identity and status within the Order. Members were no longer viewed as auxiliary members with a different Rule. Rather, by joining the rest of the Order under Saint Albert's Rule, the Secular members are recognized as an integral part of the entire Carmelite family. In many of his talks, Fr. Deeney points out the importance of understanding the Secular Order as part of the whole Order: "You are not additions to the Order of Discalced Carmelites or auxiliary members of the Order. You are an integral part of the Order." However, we should note here the two faces of the same coin—independent and distinct. The Secular Order is a distinct branch of the Order, as the Constitutions indicate. The new Constitutions expect its members to shoulder more responsibilities, "with obligations for your own government, for your own decisions, for your own formation." The Seculars, however, do not exist as an independent branch of the Order. As Fr. Deeney puts it, "distinct, yes; independent, no."

Another notable aspect of his talks is the new development in the understanding of the place of the Secular members in the Order and in the Church. The documents of the Second Vatican Council and other subsequent documents on laity—*Christifideles Laici* and *Vita Consecrata*—recognize that our vocation is ecclesial in character and we are members of the whole Church: "Your Promise is an ecclesial act. And you are more part of the Church, because you are a member of the order." The focal point of the talks is that "every vocation is ecclesial – in and for the good of the whole Church." Hence, there is a need for a greater collaboration in the apostolate of our Carmelite charism.

The highlight of the talks is the call to share with the Church and the world the spirituality of Saint Teresa of Avila and Saint John of the Cross: "How many people there are who need to know what our Carmelite Doctors of the Church have to say! If every Carmelite was dedicated to spreading Carmel's message, how many people would not be confused in the spiritual life!" We are reminded throughout the talks that "being a Carmelite is not a privilege; it is a responsibility, both personal and ecclesial." We are called to pay particular attention to paragraph 30 of *Christifideles Laici,* which highlights the basic principles of "ecclesiality" for associations and list the fruits of these principles. The first fruit listed is a renewed desire for prayer, meditation, contemplation, and the sacramental life: "These are things right down Carmel's alley."

In conclusion, let me repeat the question posed in one of the talks: "What can we do to share with others what we have received by belonging to Carmel?" The call is urgent and timely. Let us go forth and bear fruit.

Angela Pillai, OCDS
Community of Saint Joseph
Hampton, Virginia
Easter Sunday
April 11, 2009

Acknowledgments

G. K. Chesterton once said, "…thanks are the highest form of thought; and that gratitude is happiness doubled by wonder." In the spirit of wonder and gratitude, I wish to acknowledge those who have contributed in so many ways to the publication of this book.

First and foremost, my heartfelt gratitude goes to the author of this book, Fr. Aloysius Deeney, OCD, for taking many hours of his time to study and prepare for these conferences. We are grateful for his immense contribution, guidance, and sharing of his knowledge and experience with the OCDS Communities of Carmel.

I personally wish to thank Dorothy Duffy, OCDS, my dear friend and a fellow Carmelite at the Community of St. Joseph, Hampton, Virginia, for her editorial contribution and moral support. Dorothy initially introduced me to Fr. Deeney's talks with great excitement. This book is the result of her initiative and constant motivation.

I sincerely thank ICS Publications for accepting publication and distribution of this book; Br. Bryan Paquette, OCD, in particular, for sharing his expertise in the unfamiliar world of publication.

I thank both our U.S. and International communities of the Secular Order of Discalced Carmelites for their overwhelming support and enthusiasm expressed in our initial effort in introducing the talks in booklet form to the OCDS formation program. I thank you for your e-mails, cards, and letters of appreciation. The publication of this book could not have been possible without your continuous support and interest. My sincere gratitude also to one of our friends of Carmel, Joanne Re, for faithful handling of booklet distribution; keeping up with the demand of the OCDS communities and responding patiently to their needs.

Thanks be to God

Angela Pillai, OCDS

Testing and Discerning a Vocation to the Secular Order of Discalced Carmelites

The point of this presentation is to answer the question, What are the principles that you use to discern the vocation to the Secular Order of the Discalced Carmelites? Who is called to be a Secular Carmelite, and how do you distinguish between those called and those not called? Among the friars and the nuns, people do not leave because they are bad people. People are not sent home from the monastery or the convent because they are morally unacceptable. It is a vocation to be a member of the Order and one that needs, for everyone's sake, to be clearly identified. Otherwise, the Order, either the friars, or the nuns, or the seculars, loses its way and confuses its identity.

I would describe a member of the Secular Order of Our Lady of Mount Carmel and Saint Teresa of Jesus as a practicing member of the Catholic Church who, under the protection of Our Lady of Mount Carmel, and inspired by Saint Teresa of Jesus and Saint John of the Cross, makes the commitment to the Order to seek the face of God for the sake of the Church and the world.

I would note in that description six distinct elements that, coming together, are those elements that move people to approach the Order and seek identification with the Order in a more formal way.

Practicing member of the Catholic Church

"Practicing member of the Catholic Church." By this I mean Roman Catholic, not in reference to the Latin rite but in reference to the unity under the leadership of the Bishop of Rome, the Pope. The majority of Roman Catholics belong to the Latin rite. There are, however, other rites within the Roman Catholic Church: Maronite,

Malabar, Melkite, Ukrainian, etc. There are Secular Order communities in each of these rites. The OCDS community of Lebanon belongs to the Maronite rite. The word "practicing" specifies something about the person who can be a member of the Secular Order. As a basic litmus test of "practicing" the Catholic faith, I suggest the capacity to participate fully in the Eucharist with a clear conscience. The Eucharist is the summit of Catholic life and identity. It is the meeting point of heaven and earth. So, if one is free to participate in the summit, then the lesser points of participation are certainly permitted.

For most cases in the past, this was rather simple to determine. People who came to the Secular Order came from parishes where the friars were present or through contact with friars or nuns who recommended them to the Secular Order. Divorce was not a major factor in Catholic life. Most situations were clear.

It is not so today. Things are not always clear. It is precisely here where the Spiritual Assistant can be of most help to the Council of a community of the Secular Order in the screening of candidates. I give an example. A woman approaches a community of the Secular Order. The woman is known by some of the Council. They know that this is her second marriage. They also know that she regularly goes to Mass and participates in the sacraments. The Council would like clarity before admitting this person to formation.

There are a few possibilities with this case. The Church annulled the first marriage. Or, by arrangement with her confessor, she and her husband are living in such a way as to participate in the sacraments of the Church. An interview with the Spiritual Assistant would clarify the answers. Without necessity of too much explanation to respect the right to privacy and a good name that every member of the Church enjoys, he could give the word to the Council that would allow this person to enter the Secular Order.

The Secular Order is a juridical part of the Order of Discalced Carmelites. It is an institution of the Roman Catholic Church and subject to the laws of the Church. The Sacred Congregation must approve its own legislation. Therefore, someone who does not belong to the Catholic Church may not be a member of the Secular Order. Non-Catholic people with interest in the spirituality of Carmel are certainly welcome to participate in whatever way a community might invite them, but they cannot be members of the Secular Order.

Here we have the first element of the identity of a Secular Order member—a person who participates in the life of the Catholic Church. There are, of course, more, because there are millions of people who participate in the life of the Catholic Church who have not the slightest interest in Carmel.

Under the protection of Our Lady of Mount Carmel

We come to the second element—"under the protection of Our Lady of Mount Carmel." It is not just any devotion to Our Lady that identifies a person called to the Secular Order. There are many Christians who are very devoted to Our Lady and have a very highly developed Marian character to their Christian life. There are many Orthodox Christians as well as High-Church Anglicans who are very Marian. There are many Catholics who wear the scapular for all of the correct reasons and with sincere dedication to Mary who are not called to be Secular Carmelites. Not only that, but there are some people who come to the Secular Order precisely because of devotion to Mary, the scapular, and the rosary who do not have a vocation to be Secular Order members.

The particular aspect of the Blessed Virgin Mary that must be present in any person called to Carmel is that of an inclination to "meditate in the heart," the phrase that Saint Luke's Gospel uses twice to describe Mary's attitude vis-à-vis her Son. Yes, all the other aspects of Marian life and devotion can be present: devotion to the scapular, the rosary, and other things. They are, however, secondary to this aspect of Marian devotion. Mary is our model of prayer and meditation. This interest in learning to meditate or inclination to meditation is a fundamental characteristic of any OCDS. It is perhaps the most basic.

A very frequent experience of many groups is to have a person approach the Secular Order to become a member, sometimes a diocesan priest, who is very devoted to Mary, a person who has been on many pilgrimages to Marian shrines throughout the world, a person who is very familiar with many of the apparitions and messages attributed to Mary, a real authority on current Marian movements. Many times they do not have the slightest inclination to "meditate in the heart." They desire quickly to become the "teachers" of the community about the Blessed Mother and introduce an entirely un-Carmelite strain of Marian interest into the community. If this person is a priest, it is very difficult for the community to protect itself from this detour in its Marian life. There are other Marian groups and movements that might be the home for this person, but it is not the Secular Order.

In addition, within the Teresian Carmelite family, there is a place for people whose primary motivation is devotion to the scapular and Our Lady of Mount Carmel. It is the Confraternity of the Brown Scapular, or the Confraternity of Our Lady of Mount Carmel.

Mary, for a Secular Order member, is the model of a meditative attitude and disposition. She attracts and inspires a Carmelite to a contemplative way of understanding the life of the mystical body of her Son, the Church. It is she who draws the person to Carmel. And, in the formation program, which the person finds when they enter Carmel, it is this aspect that must be developed in the person. So, I say that this is the second element—"under the protection of Our Lady of Mount Carmel."

Inspired by Saint Teresa of Jesus

> *"A member of the Secular Order of Our Lady of Mount Carmel and Saint Teresa of Jesus is a practicing member of any of the rites of the Roman Catholic Church who, under the protection of Our Lady of Mount Carmel, and inspired by Saint Teresa of Jesus and Saint John of the Cross...."*

Here we have the third element. I mention both Saint Teresa of Jesus and Saint John of the Cross, and I might say, right at the beginning of this section, that I also include Saint Thérèse of the Child Jesus; Blessed Elizabeth of the Trinity or Saint Teresa Benedicta of the Cross (Edith Stein) can also be included, but Saints Teresa and John of the Cross are central to this point.

Having mentioned all of those great people of the Carmelite tradition, I underline the importance of Saint Teresa of Jesus, to whom, in our tradition we refer to as our Holy Mother. The reason is because she is the one to whom the charism was given. In many parts of the world we are called Teresian Carmelites. Saint John of the Cross was the original collaborator with our Holy Mother in both the spiritual and juridical refounding of Carmel in this new charismatic way. So he is called our Holy Father. It is hard for me to imagine any Discalced Carmelite of any brand who is not attracted by one, if not both, of these persons in their histories, personalities, and, most importantly, their writings.

The writings of Saint Teresa of Jesus are the expression of the charism of the Discalced Carmelites. The spirituality of the Discalced Carmelites has a very well-based intellectual foundation. There is a doctrine involved here. Doctrine comes from ***docere,*** Latin for "to teach." Any person who wants to be a Discalced Carmelite must be a person with an interest in learning from the teachers of Carmel. There are three Carmelinte Doctors of the Universal Church: Teresa, John, and Thérèse.

A person comes to the Community, a person with a great love of the Blessed Mother, and wants to wear the scapular in honor of Mary as a sign of dedication to her service. This person is very prayerful but has no interest in reading or studying the spirituality of the Teresian Carmel. This person tries to read one of the Carmelite Doctors but just cannot find the interest to keep reading. To me, this is a good person who may belong in the Confraternity of the Brown Scapular, but definitely does not have a vocation to the Secular Order of Carmel.

There is an academic aspect to the formation of a Teresian Carmelite. There is an intellectual basis to the spirituality and identity of one who is called to the Order. And, as with each friar and each nun, each Secular represents the Order. A Carmelite who does not have the interest in studying or deepening the roots of his/her identity through prayer and study loses their identity and can no longer represent the Order. Nor does that person speak for the Order. Many times, when listening to a Carmelite speak, it becomes obvious when hearing what is said that they have not gone beyond what they heard in formation years before.

This intellectual basis is the beginning of an attitude that is open to study. It leads to a deeper interest in Scripture, theology, and the documents of the Church. The tradition of spiritual reading, *Lectio Divina,* and time for study are the intellectual backbone of the spiritual life. Good formation depends on good information. When the information is bad or absent or incorrect, the formation stops or is stunted, resulting in confusion in the Secular. If that Secular, through some twist of fate, becomes somehow an officer of the OCDS Community, the Community suffers. It happens with friars and nuns, and it happens with Seculars.

This academic or intellectual basis is very important and has been sadly missing in many groups of the Secular Order. It is not a question of "being an intellectual" in order to be a Secular. It is a question of being intelligent in the pursuit of the truth about God, about oneself, about prayer, about the Order, and about the Church. Obedience has long been associated with the intellect and the virtue of faith. Obedience, meaning openness to hearing (*ob* + *audire* in Latin), is a radical attitude of the person to move beyond what that person knows. Education also comes from Latin (*ex* + *ducere,* to lead out of). Saint Teresa describes the person of the third mansions as almost stuck and unable to move. One of the characteristics of such people, permanently in the third mansions, is that they want to teach everybody else. They know it all. In reality, they are disobedient and uneducable; that is, they are closed and unable to learn.

Commitment to the Order

The fourth element of the description is "who makes the commitment to the Order." There are so many committed Catholics who are devoted to Mary and even experts in Saint Teresa, Saint John of the Cross—or one of our saints—who do not have the vocation to the Secular Order. These people may be contemplatives or even hermits, who spend hours in prayer and study each day, but do not have the vocation to be a Carmelite. What is the element that differentiates these people from those called to follow Christ more closely as Secular Carmelites?

It is neither the spirituality nor the study nor the devotion to

Mary. Simply put, the Secular Carmelite is moved to commit himself or herself to the Order and to the Church. This commitment, in the form of the Promises, is an ecclesial event and an event of the Order in addition to being an event in the life of the person who makes the Promises. In a certain sense, remembering always the person's context of family, work, and responsibilities that are involved in his/her life, the person who commits him/herself, becomes characterized as a Carmelite.

As I said, it is an ecclesial event and an event of the Order. It is for this reason that the Church and the Order have the essential say, in union with the candidate, in accepting and approving the commitment of the person. It is also for this reason that the Church and the Order give the conditions and set the terms for the content of the Promises. A person may want to commit him/herself to certain things, daily meditation or the Divine Office, for example. But the Church, through the Order, establishes the basic and broad lines of understanding with regard to this commitment.

The Secular belongs to Carmel. Carmel does not belong to the Secular. What I mean by that is that there is a new identity, one developed from the baptismal identity, which becomes a necessary point of reference. As the Church is the point of reference for the baptized person (the baptized person belongs to the Church), so Carmel becomes the point of reference for the Secular. The more "Catholic" one becomes, the more one recognizes the catholicity of the Church. The more one becomes Carmelite, the more one recognizes the catholicity of Carmel as well. In fact, the person who commits him/herself to Carmel in the Secular Order discovers that Carmel becomes essential to his/her identity as a Catholic. It is because the Promises are the means by which one becomes a Secular Order member that formation for the Promises is so important—formation and ongoing formation.

An important aspect to this commitment is the commitment to the community. A person who wishes to be a member of the OCDS must be able to form community, be a part of a group that is dedicated to a common goal, show interest in the other members, be supportive in the pursuit of a life of prayer, and be able to receive the support of others. This applies even to those persons who for various reasons cannot actively participate in a Community. In the formation of the future of the Community, this social characteristic is one that should develop. There are many people who are introverted and quiet, but who are still quite sociable and capable of forming Communities. And there are many people who are quite extroverted and at the same time incapable of forming Community. In this question it is necessary to use common sense. Answer the question, What will this person help the Community to be in ten years?

There is also the question of people who belong to other movements—for example the New Catechumemate, Focolare, Marian Movement of Priests, and Charismatic Renewal. If a person's involvement in other movements does not interfere with that person's commitment to Carmel and that person does not introduce elements that are not compatible with OCDS spirituality to the Community, then there is generally no problem. It is when the person distracts the Community from its own purpose and style of spiritual life that problems begin. Sometimes there are people so confused that they come to Carmel and talk about Our Lady of Medjugorie and go to a Medjugorie meeting and talk about Teresian prayer.

The most important point is that the person must choose the Secular Order, and that commitment ought to be more important than other movements or groups.

This commitment to the Church through Carmel has both content and purpose. These are expressed in the final two elements of my description of who is a Secular Carmelite.

To seek the face of God.

The fifth element of the description is "to seek the face of God." This element expresses the content of the Promises. I could rephrase this element in various ways, "to pray," "to meditate," and "to live the spiritual life." I have chosen this one because it is scriptural and expresses the nature of contemplation—a wondering observation of God's word and work in order to know, love, and serve him. The contemplative aspect of Carmelite life focuses on God, recognizing always that contemplation is a gift of God, not an acquisition as a result of putting in sufficient time. This is the commitment to personal holiness. The OCDS wants to see God, wants to know God, and recognizes that prayer and meditation now take on a greater importance. The Promises are a commitment to a new way of life in which "allegiance to Jesus Christ" marks the person and the way this person lives.

The personal life of the Secular Carmelite becomes contemplative. The style of life changes with the growth in the virtues that accompany the growth in the Spirit. It is impossible to live a life of prayer, meditation, and study without changing. This new style of life enhances all the rest of life. The majority of Secular Order members who are married, and those with families, experience that the commitment to the OCDS life enriches their marital and familial commitment. Men and women OCD Seculars who work experience a new moral commitment to justice in the workplace. Those who are single, widowed, or separated find in this commitment to holiness a source of grace and strength to live their lives with dedication and purpose. This is the direct result of seeking the face of God.

Is the essence of Carmel prayer? Many times I have heard or read that affirmation. I am never sure just how to answer that. Not because I do not know what prayer is or because prayer is not of great importance for any Carmelite, but because I never know what the speaker or writer wishes to justify by the statement. If the person means by prayer personal holiness and the pursuit of a genuine spirituality that recognizes the supremacy of God and of God's will for the human family, then yes, I agree. If the person means that I as a Carmelite fulfill my entire obligation as a Carmelite by being faithful to my prayer and that there is nothing else that I need do, then no, I do not agree. Personal holiness is not the same as a personal pursuit of holiness. For a baptized member of the Church, holiness is always ecclesial, never self-centered or self-content. I am never the judge of my own holiness. *(Nemo judex in causo suo.)*

I am sanctified by the practice of the virtues, which is the direct result of a life of prayerful searching for God's will in my life. This is the Carmelite secret—prayer does not make us holy. Prayer is the essential element in Christian (Carmelite) holiness because it is the frequent contact necessary to remain faithful to God. This contact allows God to do his will in my life, which then announces to the whole world God's presence and goodness. Without the contact of prayer, I cannot know God and God cannot be known to others.

To seek the face of God requires an unbelievable amount of discipline in the classic and original sense of the word—disciple, one who learns. I must recognize that I am forever a student. Never do I become a master. I am always surprised by what God does in the world. God is forever a mystery. The clues to God's existence always interest me. I find them in the events of life, single, widowed, married, family, work, and retirement. But they only become recognizable and clear through prayer, observing from the heart. The call to holiness is a burning desire in the heart and mind of the one called to the Secular Order. It is a commitment that the Secular must make. The Secular is drawn to prayer, finding in prayer a home and an identity.

This prayer, this pursuit of holiness, and this encounter with the Lord make the Secular more part of the Church. And, as a more committed member of the Church, the Secular's life is more ecclesial. As the life of prayer grows, it produces more fruit in the person's personal life (the growth of virtue) and in the person's ecclesial life (apostolate).

For the sake of the Church and the world

This leads me to the sixth element of the description "for the sake of the Church and the world." This is the newest development in the understanding of the place of the Secular in the Order and in the Church. This is the result of the development in the theology of the Church on the role of laypersons in the Church and applying that theology to the Order. Beginning with the Second Vatican Council's document *On the Apostolate of the Laity* and its fruition with the Synods on the Laity in 1986 and the Consecrated Life in 1996 (*Christifideles Laici* and *Vita Consecrata*), the Church has constantly underlined the need for a further commitment of the laity to her needs and the needs of the world. Saint Teresa had the conviction that the only proof of prayer was growth in virtue and that the necessary fruit of the life of prayer was the birth of good works.

At times I hear a Secular say: "The only apostolate of the Secular is prayer." The word that makes that statement false is "only." A prayerful and obedient attitude toward the documents of the Church makes it clear that the role of the layperson within the Church has changed. The Rule of Life talked about the need of each Secular to have an individual apostolate. *Christifideles Laici* highlights the importance of group apostolates of associations in the Church, and the OCDS is an association in the Church. Many Seculars, when they hear the mention of group apostolate, think that I am talking about the entire community being involved in something that takes up hours each day. That is not at all what "group apostolate" means. Paragraph 30 of *Christifideles Laici* gives the basic principles of "ecclesiality" for associations and lists the fruits of these principles. The first fruit listed is a renewed desire for prayer, meditation, contemplation, and the sacramental life. These are things "right down Carmel's alley." How many people there are who need to know what our Carmelite Doctors of the Church have to say! If every Carmelite was dedicated to spreading Carmel's message, how many people would not be confused in the spiritual life! Walk into any major bookstore and see what nonsense is listed in the section entitled "mysticism."

Each Community ought to answer the question as a Community, What can we do to share with others what we have received by belonging to Carmel?

We, as Carmelites, can help to clean up the mess by making known what we know. It is not an option. It is a responsibility. Being a Carmelite is not a privilege; it is a responsibility, both personal and ecclesial.

As I said at the beginning, it is not any one element that discerns the person who has the vocation to Carmel as a Secular. It is the combination that makes the difference.

The New OCDS Legislation and the Vocation to Carmel

For 800 years there has been only one document in the tradition of Carmel that goes by the title "Rule." That document is the Rule of Saint Albert. That Rule, together with the Rules of Saint Augustine, Saint Benedict, Saint Francis of Assisi, and Saint Dominic for the Western Church and Saint Basil for the Eastern Church, have been the official guides for religious families since the 1200s.

The Rule of Saint Albert is the one document that all Carmelites of both the OCarm and OCD traditions have in common.

The OCD friars have as official legislation the Rule of Saint Albert and the Constitutions approved by the Holy See, which serve as a way to live the spirituality of the Rule for current times.

The OCD nuns have as official legislation the Rule of Saint Albert and the Constitutions approved by the Holy See, which serve as a way to live the spirituality of the Rule for current times.

The OCD seculars have had a different development in history. They are not an independent branch of Carmel. As the Constitutions recognize in article 41, they are a dependent branch of the Order but with a distinct identity.

The Constitutions that you now have as your legislation are not the Rule of Life, which was written in 1974. These Constitutions are a development and evolution of what the Secular Order is.

The Secular Order started some 600 years ago when Blessed John Soreth with his Council and with the friars decided that this spirituality that had been developed from Isreal, from the Holy Land into Europe and was developing into the mendicant life, should be shared. So the decision was made to establish the order of nuns and the Secular Order. Prior to the end of 1400, there were only Carmelite friars. So, your history as Secular members of the Order, although that was not always clearly understood and still is not clearly understood, is that you are members of the Order.

The Secular Order groups that began 600 years ago were generally groups of laypeople who over the next 500 years to the early 1900s were identified with a monastery of friars. Only in the early 1900s did the Secular Order groups begin in places that were not associated with monasteries of friars and so there was generally the idea that the nuns had a particular identity because they lived in monasteries and the friars had a particular identity because they were friars who lived in monasteries. The Secular members were, in fact and in understanding, auxiliary or adjunct members to the monasteries of friars. And that's generally how they were understood.

During the course of history, before 1921, there were various regulations in different parts of Europe that guided the OCDS or Third-Order Carmelites according to countries. There were different rules in different parts of the world because the Secular Order was not understood as a global entity. But even those many rules were a step forward in understanding the Seculars as a group of laypeople who had legislation of some kind. Legislation gives identity; it establishes you as distinct. In 1918, a new Code of Canon law went into effect, and one of the results of this new law was that religious communities had to identify the laypeople who were associated with them. Which of these groups were confraternities and which of these groups actually formed some part of the Order? The "Order," at that time, was understood to mean the friars and the nuns.

In 1918, at the request of the General in Rome, the Secular Order had the first attempt at a common legislation, which was called the Manual. This first attempt at a universal and common legislation was a result of the first Code of Canon Law, which became obligatory in 1918.

After the Second Vatican Council in 1974, the Order asked a committee of friars from different parts of the world to update the Manual. The result was the publication in 1974 of the document known as the Rule of Life. It was finally approved in 1979. Of course, the Manual ceased to be valid because the Church approved the Rule of Life.

The word "Rule" used with this document was perhaps a misnomer because it may have caused confusion with the Rule of Saint Albert.

In any case, this legislation in 1979 was followed by a number of documents of the Church that necessitated a new approach. Those documents were the New Code of Canon Law (1983); *Christifideles Laici* (1987), following the Synod on Laypersons in the Church; and *Vita Consacrata* (1997), following the Synod on Consecrated Life.

As a result of these documents it was mandatory for the Order to look at the legislation of the Secular members and bring that legislation into line with the law and theology those documents expressed.

Recognizing the place of Secular members within the family and Order of Carmel, it became understood that like the friars and nuns, it was time for the Secular Order members to have as official legislation—the Rule of Saint Albert and the Constitutions approved by the Holy See that serve as a way to live the spirituality of the Rule for current times.

These Constitutions, submitted to the Holy See, were approved finally and definitively in June 2003. The Constitutions replace entirely the Rule of Life as the Rule of Life replaced entirely the Manual. Anyone, priest or layperson, Carmelite or non-Carmelite, who says differently is entirely mistaken. Are these Constitutions infallible or irreplaceable? Absolutely not. It will be necessary to redo them again in another thirty, forty, or fifty years. Why is that? That is because the nature of Constitutions is to help the members (friars, nuns, and seculars) to live the spirituality of the Order in response to the needs of the world as the Church indicates and demands.

Most of us are familiar with that Rule of Life and now are becoming familiar with the Constitutions. However, most of us still think in terms of the Rule of Life in our understanding because that is what we were trained in. The Constitutions are another step forward in the identity of the Secular Carmelite.

Our Identity, Values, and Commitment

The identity is highlighted in the Preface of the Constitutions:

"The great Teresian Carmelite family is present in the world in many forms. The nucleus of this family is the Order of Discalced Carmelites: the Friars, the Nuns, and the Seculars. It is the one Order with the same charism. The Order is nourished by the long tradition of Carmel, expressed in the Rule of St. Albert and the doctrine of the Carmelite Doctors of the Church and the Order's other saints."

"Secular Carmelites, together with the Friars and Nuns, are sons and daughters of the Order of Our Lady of Mt. Carmel and St. Teresa of Jesus. As a result, they share the same charism with the religious each according to their particular state of life. It is one family with the same spiritual possessions, the same call to holiness (Ep 1:4; 1P 1:15) and the same apostolic mission. Secular members contribute to the Order the benefits proper to their secular state" (*Lumen Gentium* 31—*Christifideles Laici* 9—*The Lay Members of Christ's Faithful People—Apostolie Exhortation of John Paul II*).

Members of the Church

"The members of the Secular Order of Discalced Carmelites are faithful members of the Church called to live 'in allegiance to Jesus

Christ' through a friendship with the One we know loves us in service to the Church. Under the protection of Our Lady of Mount Carmel, in the biblical tradition of the prophet Elijah and inspired by the teachings of St. Teresa of Jesus and St. John of the Cross, they seek to deepen their Christian commitment received in Baptism."

Now your identity in these Constitutions, approved by the Holy See, is confirmed. You are not adjunct members of the Order. You are not auxiliary to the Order. You are the Order. The Secular Order is present in countries where there are no friars and no nuns, and it is amazing how fast it is growing. There are 40,000 Secular Order members in ninety countries. It has now developed into a presence within the Order.

One of the things I'm most frequently asked for is a formation program. But I believe the request is actually, What do we do in the first year, second year, third year, fourth year, and fifth year? Rather than a formation program, they want to know what is the information they are supposed to give. I had one developed, but I was a little hesitant to give it out because we are not clear about what the formation program should be.

One of the glaring empty spots in most formation programs that I have seen is that there is very little emphasis given in formation to the very thing that makes you members of the Secular Order: the Promise. It is this that makes you members of the Secular Order—not Saint Teresa of Jesus, not Saint John of the Cross, and not the spirituality of how to pray or how to use the Bible for *Lectio Divina.* There are many people who use all those things who are not members of the Order. And because this formation for the Promise is lacking, many times people do not understand themselves as members of the Order. They understand themselves as Carmelites, but not as members of the Order. I am a member of the Order because I belong to a Province that received me, in which I made my commitment; therefore, I'm a Carmelite, because I'm incorporated.

Another area that is lacking in the formation programs is imparting a true understanding of community. You are members of the Order because you belong to a community, because you identify with other people who share your identity and in that sharing confirm each other.

To illustrate this point, I want to respond to a question that I am very frequently asked. I want to respond, give an explanation, and make a suggestion. The question comes from Presidents or Council members, but mostly from Formation Directors: "Father, what do we do about people who come to the Secular Order but belong to many other organizations—they go to Charismatic meetings, they go to Cenacle meetings, also belong to Medjugorje prayer groups and belong to Our Lady speaks to beloved priests, and they belong to all those things. How do we explain to them that this is different than belonging to all those different things?"

I try to be practical in answering that question. What are the obligations these Constitutions envision in the life of the Secular Order Member? I see six obligations that are part of the rhythm of the Secular Carmelite's life. These six obligations consume time and energy.

1. Meditation.

Carmel is identified with meditation. I'm using the word meditation as opposed to the word contemplation because we know that most of us wait a long time before God gives us the gift of contemplation. So we meditate or do mental prayer if you would like to use that term. Meditation is our daily devotion under the inspiration of Our Lady of Mount Carmel, who is our Lady of Meditation—it's that way of relating to God that is specific to Carmel and Carmel's love, devotion, and relationship with God. So I put that in first place because we can do that no matter where we are. Traditionally, we use about thirty minutes a day. It might be fifteen minutes in the morning and fifteen minutes in the afternoon, or it might be thirty minutes at one time. Sometimes it might be ten minutes three times a day depending on work or family schedules and other things. We have to be practical, but we are conscious of having to do that. We are conscious of wanting to do that. Common sense—that's the Carmelite spirituality. Meditation is in the first place as the first of our daily obligations that takes thirty minutes of our day. Part III on the Constitutions: Witnesses to the Experience of God, pp. 17–24, is entirely on prayer.

2. Morning Prayer, Evening Prayer, and, if you can, Night Prayer.

Night Prayer, as the Constitutions mention, is optional. All of these things are when you can do it. If you can't do it, you can't do it! None of these things that I mention are under the obligation of sin, except what the Church commends as under the obligation of sin. The friars and the nuns have two hours of mental prayer a day—an hour in the morning and one hour in the evening; our Office of Readings, Morning Prayer, Mid-day Prayer, Evening Prayer, Night Prayer—the nuns have two more hours of prayer. Why do we have more and you have less? Why? Because you have families, or you have jobs and other obligations that God is going to ask you about first.

Here are two reasons why I think it important to emphasize the Liturgy of Hours as prayer. First, when we said Morning Prayer this morning, the Pope in Rome said the same exact Morning Prayer nine hours before. The Secular Order members in Malaysia said them six hours before that. When you are at home by yourself and you are saying Morning Prayer or Evening Prayer or Night Prayer, you are not doing that alone, you are joining other people.

The second reason is you are not picking texts that are pleasing to you; that's not prayer, that's self-consolation. How can you hope to convert to the will of God if you are making the word of God convert to how you feel? You are taking texts that the Church says, offers, and gives, and you are adjusting your spirit to it. So we use the Liturgy of Hours to get us out of ourselves with the words of the Holy Spirit in the Scriptures and prayer. So Morning Prayer, Evening Prayer, and Night Prayer would probably take twenty-five minutes out of our day. Add that to the thirty minutes for mental prayer and we have fifty-five minutes of our day used up.

3. Mass.

Of course, Mass is the most important thing in the hierarchy of order. But we have to go some place to do that. For Morning Prayer, Evening Prayer, Night Prayer, or Meditation, we can do it on a plane, we can do it at home, or we can do it on the way to work. We don't have to go to Church to do those things. But if we go to Mass with some frequency, more than once a week, more than Sunday, which is an obligation, by the time you get up, leave, you drive to Church, go to Mass, drive home, we're talking, at a minimum, forty-five minutes to an hour or more time. So that's thirty minutes for Mental Prayer, plus twenty-five minutes for the Liturgy of the Hours, plus forty-five for Mass or an hour and forty minutes.

4. Mary.

We're a Marian Order of the Church, and there may be some expression of devotion to Mary that we want to practice every day, if we can. Our first and primary devotion to Mary, however, is expressed in meditation, looking as Mary did, in St. Luke's Gospel twice, at the life of Christ and meditating on these things in her heart. That's our primary Marian devotion. We wear the scapular. Many people say the Rosary every day. So let's add another fifteen minutes to say the Rosary, for those who say the Rosary. It's not mandatory. The Rosary is an expression of devotion. If you do say the Rosary, there's another fifteen minutes, so you have an hour and fifty-five minutes every day, and we still have two M's to go!

This is what we are trying to explain to people when they come to the Secular Order or to people in the Secular Order as to what we are, what they are doing when they are joining this. What are their obligations? Those first four things: Meditation, Morning Prayer, Mass, Mary—they are a part of the personal daily life of the individual member of the Secular Order. The other two M's are a little bit different because they are not a part of the daily life but a part of the energy flow, you might say, of the Secular Order members.

5. Meetings.

There are so many things that fit into this category of meetings: formation, information, and fellowship. Formation—not just the formation of individuals but also the formation of community as a community. It is not a collective group of individuals who love our Lady and love Carmelite spirituality. It is a community of people who have made a commitment to each other. It's very clear, when you make your promises, you make it to the Community. You are incorporating yourselves as members of a Community.

Another important understanding that is mentioned in the Constitutions is that the Spiritual Assistant is not meant to be Formation Director for the Community because it is not his job to form individual members of the Community. His job, as defined in the Constitutions, is to support and assist the President, the Council, and the Formation Director.

That is part of forming community because if the leadership of the Community understands their responsibility and their role, then the Community begins to take shape and it's identity becomes clear as a community of people. The Council has to function properly, and all must realize that the Council is the superior of the Community, not the President. The superior of the Council is the Provincial, and the superior of the Provincial is the General.

But in order for the Council to function properly, it has to function in a certain way. It has to be educated, formed to function as the leadership of the Community. When we speak about the formation of the Council, there are some things that have to be understood about Councils and the way they function. If you are a member of the Council, you have an obligation to the other members of the Council and to the Community to respect the privacy of the Council.

If a member of the Council reveals, outside of the Council, decisions that have been made regarding candidates or other important matters, it could result in divisions within the Community and stifle the freedom that Councilors should feel within the Council meetings. How can the Council arrive at a good decision if Councilors are afraid to speak, afraid to express themselves because they are afraid that their opinion is going to be repeated? Confidentiality is a practical and necessary point.

There is also the necessity for information. We call them formation classes, but I'm going to call them "information classes." where information is passed on in the various stages of those being formed. Remember that there are three stages in initial formation: those in the Aspirancy, those in the two years preparing for First Promises, and those in the three-year period before Definitive Promises. I hope that in those two years prior to First Promises that there is enough preparation for the importance of the Promise and what it means. Not just what does Saint Teresa teach about prayer and how to use the Bible—I'm repeating this again because it is a very important point, to understand the consequences of making the Promises. Then in the third period of formation for three years, there is the preparation for the Final Promises. So, there are different stages of information that need to be given. And they can't all be given at once. You can't put people who are in the Aspirancy stage together with those who are preparing for Definitive Promises.

In some Communities, I have found that everybody from the oldest to the youngest, including those who have made Definitive Promises, are all together for the formation program. That's not really good formation. You can't put people who are in the Aspirancy stage in with those who are in Definitive Promises. If I'm a teacher of mathematics and I put first graders in with eighth graders, it would not work for obvious reasons. Paragraph 36 of the Constitutions states very clearly that there is a "gradual introduction to the life of the Secular Order structure…." So it's important to understand that it is done in stages. It is a gradual introduction to the life of the Secular Order.

The purpose of the Aspirancy is to give the Community an opportunity to make an adequate discernment of the person who is coming. "After the initial period of contact the Council of the Community 'may' admit the applicant to a more serious period of formation that usually last for two years leading up to the first promises"(Constituions VI: 35b). Our Communities are not factories of Carmelites, where we put people on a conveyor belt to form them, and once you have finished the Aspirancy period, you have to enter into the second period automatically. How can that be good formation?

So the Constitutions specifically say that it is the Councils responsibility to decide if the person is ready to begin the next stage, and the Council might not be ready or the person may not be ready.

So does that mean that they either go home or they have to begin the next stage? No, it may be necessary to add a few extra months. If you have a fixed time, for example, six months or twelve months for Aspirancy, you can lengthen it by one half of the original time, either three or six months depending on your term of Aspirancy. Same with the second period where there is two years, you can lengthen it by one year. The third period of three years can be lengthened by one and a half years. This will be helpful for our communities because then they will take extra care in making decisions and in informing and forming our people.

"At the end of this stage, with the approval of the Council of the Community, the applicant may be invited to make the First Promises"(Constitutions VI:35c). So, with the approval, the applicant "may" be—see the language that is used in here—it's not necessary that they be invited to make the promises after two years.

And, "In the last three years of the initial formation, there is a deeper study of prayer, the Scriptures, Documents of the Church, the saints of the order and formation in the Apostolate of the Order. At the end of these three years, the applicant may be invited by the Council to make Definitive Promises" (Constitutions VI:35d).

One of the differences between the Constitutions versus the Rule of Life is that in the Rule, the Spiritual Assistant had the right to veto the decision of the Council to admit someone to the various stages of formation. That's gone. The Council now has the responsibility of making those decisions and carrying out those decisions. We are not just forming individuals, but we are forming Communities. Is this person capable of being a member of your Community? Not are they capable of praying; not are they capable of saying the Rosary every day; not if they are very faithful to Mass everyday;—but are they capable of being members of your Community? Are they capable of relating to the other people in the Community?

This is again a step forward in the understanding of the Discalced Carmelite Secular Order member's vocation. You have Community. It is one thing to know the Carmelite Spirituality and another thing to be a member of the Order. They are two different things. Hopefully, members of the Order know the spirituality, but there are experts on the spirituality who are not members of the Order, who do not know what it means to be a member of the Order. They may know Saint Teresa and Saint John of the Cross and be able to quote them better than most of us, but that doesn't mean they know what it means to be a Carmelite. You are Carmelites. We are Carmelites. The nuns are Carmelites.

So being part of a Community, being involved in forming that Community is what happens at the meetings. Because you, Secular Order members, have meetings where you meet and talk with other people, and you decide things about your Carmelite life together and are responsible for forming yourselves as members of this religious family. Your part in that now is very much to take responsibility. In my visits with Communities around the world, I've discovered that there are many Communities of the Secular Order who have no idea of belonging to the Order.

It's not because those priests who formed them did not understand something about Carmelite spirituality; they did understand something about Carmelite spirituality, but they did not understand what it meant to be a member of the Order.

An example is Thailand. There are two Secular Order Communities—one is very large, it has about 120 members. I'm the first Discalced Carmelite priest they've seen as Secular Order members. It has taken me three visits before they finally began to understand that I am coming from Rome because they belong to what I belong to. They had no contact with the Order. They have a diocesan priest who is very good, who studies their spirituality and knows a lot about Carmelite spirituality, but even he did not understand that Secular Order members were members of the Order.

So, formation, information, fellowship—these are the three things that happen in meetings. Without these meetings your Order falls apart; your Communities fall apart. People who do not come to meetings cease to be members, even if they are still on the rolls.

6. Mission.

Paragraph 25 of the Constitutions speaks of the realization on the part of the religious orders that because of the events in history, there is a need to share not only the spirituality but also the mission of the Order. I've come to use the word "mission" instead of the word "apostolate," because when I use the word "apostolate," people tend to get nervous. They say, "Am I supposed to quit my job and leave my family?" So I use the word "mission."

Carmel has a mission. Carmel's mission is that we know God so that God may be known. That's the gift of our vocation. That is what we receive by being Carmelites: we know God. But it's not just for us; it's so that God may be known. There is a fairly new two-volume book of the Concordances on the writings of Saint Teresa in Spanish. Eight hundred and ten times in the Concordance, Saint Teresa uses the verb "to serve" in Spanish to describe the life of prayer. We are Teresian Carmelites. Do not have some fantastic image of Saint Teresa that removes her from service—from doing for others for God.

When I went to be a Carmelite, I thought I'd be off in a cloister someplace praying. I didn't know who was going to do the dishes, but I was sure I was going to pray. There's that quote from Saint Teresa that says that works is what the Lord wants, works. She is saying this to cloistered nuns. The reason that God is giving us grace to know him through the life of prayer is for us to do something. We cannot do it without prayer. In the Constitutions, Chapter 3 is entirely on prayer.

Chapter 4 is then Serving God's Plan. The verb used "serving" is on purpose—it's a Teresian verb and is used when talking about the prayer life. If she uses it 810 times in writing about the life of prayer, there must be something very specific about that verb. The mission that you share in is to know God—the Carmelite interior life—so that God may be made known. That's our Carmelite mission (Apostolate). When I speak about the mission of the Secular Order, I speak of doing something as a community, especially together with the Friars in terms of helping to spread Carmelite spirituality.

So Meditation; Morning Prayer, Evening Prayer, Night Prayer, Mass; Mary; Meetings and Mission: these six things are an answer to people who want to become a Carmelite, who also belong to many other groups. If they want to be a Carmelite, this is what is entailed. It is a sacrifice to do these things every day, to have this as a rhythm in your life. It takes time and commitment and leaves little time for other groups if you are going to do it well. Some people have the club mentality with regard to religious organizations, but this is not a club. You don't join a club when you become a member of the Order.

So I want to make a suggestion for a comment to be included in the Provincial Statues. "All are welcome to become members of the Secular Order except those who belong to other Secular Orders, and/or those who belong to other organizations whose membership would prohibit the person from participating fully in the life of the Secular Order." That's Teresian! Again, the step forward in these Constitutions is a step forward in the understanding of the Secular Order as members of the Order. That step forward has to be developed in the communities. We must strive to develop an understanding of our corporate identity, to develop the understanding of belonging to this body of the Order. We the friars and you yourselves have treated yourselves as individuals in many ways. But the structure that's given in the Constitutions of the Secular Order now understands you as members with responsibilities and with obligations for your own government, for your own decisions, for your own formation. And it's part of the way the Holy Spirit is moving the Church along.

I've repeated many times "member of the Order" because I want to put emphasis on the fact that you are Carmelites because you are members of the Order. This is not joining a club. And, as I've said many times before, "being a Carmelite is not a privilege. Being a Carmelite is a responsibility!" That's for me and for you. Responsibility doesn't mean burden—it means the ability to respond. So, as Carmelites, we are given the grace of our vocation through those six means to respond to the God who calls us and to respond to the world that needs to know God.

A New Vision—Apostolate of Our Charism

It is not my task to present the theories or principles of Carmelite spirituality or the theology of the Church on the role of laypersons. The purpose of my talk is to present some of the practical aspects of those principles and propose possibilities for a new vision of the Secular Order as that vision might be expressed in a constitutional form.

I would like to begin with two quotes, one from our Holy Mother, Saint Teresa of Jesus, and the second from an Anglican priest, very devoted to Teresian-Sanjuanist spirituality. Teresa in the seventh mansions states "This is the reason for prayer, my daughters, the purpose of this spiritual matrimony, the birth always of good works, of good works."

Truman Dickens, an Anglican priest, wrote a book, the purpose of which he expressed in the preface. He said that he wanted his book *The Crucible of Love,* a synopsis of Teresian and Sanjuanist spirituality, not to be just another theoretical dissertation on the spiritual life, but he wanted to make a practical contribution to "the most urgent pastoral problem of our times: to teach our people to pray."

Keep those two thoughts in mind: Saint Teresa says that the purpose of prayer is the birth of good works, and Truman Dickens says that the most urgent pastoral problem is to teach people to pray.

Teresian Charism

It is necessary to recognize that the Teresian Carmelite charism is lived in three distinct styles of life. What are these styles of life? The life of the friars, of the nuns, and of the laypersons, who by ecclesial commitment form the one Order known as the Discalced Carmelites.

The Teresian charism is one and is distinct from the style of life in which it is lived in each branch.

The vocation of the friars is contemplative, mendicant, and apostolic. It is mendicant in that the friars are obliged to live in Communities that form parts of a Province but not obliged to one specific monastery. They can be moved within the Province or to other Provinces for various reasons. And the friars are apostolic in that they exercise ministries in the service of the Church. Those friars who are ordained are obliged by ordination to exercise sacramental ministry and to preach the word.

The vocation of the nuns is contemplative, monastic, and cloistered, and from the monastic cloister they exercise their apostolate. Their style of life is monastic in that they commit themselves for life to one monastery. They are not transferred except for the rarest of causes or to make a new foundation. They are cloistered in that they are obliged by the laws of the Church to observe papal enclosure. The specific apostolate that the nuns exercise is that of the service of prayer for the Church.

The vocation of the secular is contemplative, lay and apostolic. It is lay in that the secular is called to live in the world in the community of the proper family in most cases or in a single state of life and are called to form Communities with other seculars who have the same Carmelite vocation. It is apostolic in all of the senses that the Second Vatican Council and Pope John Paul II have emphasized in the documents *Apostolicam Actuositatem and Christifideles Laici.* The vocation to be a Carmelite deepens and directs the call to personal sanctity, so that personal sanctity becomes the means to exercise an apostolic service in the world.

The nuns, the friars, and the seculars all have one common vocation: to realize personal sanctification through the charismatic tradition of Teresa of Jesus and John of the Cross. This personal sanctification then becomes the source of graces and gifts for the Church, the basis of apostolic service. Apostolic service is a necessary fruit of personal sanctification. Without apostolic service, the efforts of the friar or the nun or the secular to be holy become frustrated. What we do not have in common is the style of life in which that realization takes place. One possible identification of the Teresian charism might be the following: inspired by the life and teaching of Saint Teresa of Jesus, to seek the face of God so as to be of service to the Church and the world.

It is necessary to distinguish well between contemplation and cloister. A common misunderstanding is to think that the nuns are the true Carmelites because they are cloistered and the rest of us do our best to imitate them, but always in some watered-down version. It is not true. The Teresian Carmelite charism is ecclesial. Teresa, John, and Thérèse are Doctors of the Universal Church, because their teaching applies to the Universal Church and is not confined to the world of the cloister. The nuns are not imitation friars or seculars, the friars are not imitation nuns or seculars, and the seculars are not imitation friars or nuns. The grace of our vocation is to be Carmelite in every way possible.

In a broad way, and for the purpose of making this distinction, I would venture to say that most cloistered persons are still waiting for the grace of contemplation, and the greatest majority of contemplatives do not live in cloisters. All Carmelites of whatever style of life or vocational state are called to "meditate day and night on the law of the Lord." This is a responsibility imposed by the charism, but more importantly, born of the interior needs of our vocation. I would say that this need to "meditate on the law of the Lord" is precisely the interior impetus that brought us to Carmel. The cloister of the nuns is a requirement of the Church put in place as a means to protect the style of life in which the nuns perfect their response to the Lord's call. God has a purpose for calling us to this vocation.

God Has a Purpose for Calling Us to this Vocation.

The writings of Saint Teresa and the other Carmelite authors confirm that God has a purpose for calling us to this meditation. And God's purposes always take us out of ourselves and beyond our intentions. In the discernment of a vocation within the Church and within the Order, there are always two questions that need to be asked. The first question is, Why do you want to be a Carmelite? Each one of us, friar, nun, or secular, has our individual and personal response to that question. The second question is, Why does God want you to be a Carmelite? The answer to that question comes from an understanding of the teaching of the Church on the different states of life of baptized persons. Applying this to the vocation to be a secular, the identity of the layperson within the Church and the understanding of the Order of the place of laypersons in this religious family must be clearly understood. The answer to this second question is not personal and individual. It is "institutional" in the sense that the answer comes from outside the person. The answer comes from the Order. This second question and answer purify our personal motives and perfects them so that what God wants is done. It is also a lifelong process.

The Call of the Church

In order to better know how to read the Teresian charism in the context of the needs of the Church and the world of the twenty-first century, I think it would be helpful to cite the call of the Church expressed in the Synod on the Laity and the post synodal document *Christifideles Laici*. There are three specific texts that are helpful here.

The first is a definition of the expression "charism."

"Whether they be exceptional and great or simple and ordinary, the charisms are graces of the Holy Spirit that have, directly or indirectly, a usefulness for the ecclesial community, ordered as they are to the building up of the Church, to the well-being of humanity and to the needs of the world" (CL, 24). If our vocation as Carmelites is a true charism of the Holy Spirit, and it is, and the Church recognizes it as such, then we must ask ourselves and express ourselves in our legislation as to how precisely our ecclesial charism is useful for "building up the Church, the well-being of humanity and the needs of the world" (CL, 24).

The second is the specific reference to those lay groups juridically identified with religious families.

> In recent days the phenomenon of lay people associating among themselves has taken on a character of particular variety and vitality. In some ways lay associations have always been present throughout the Church's history as various confraternities, third orders and sodalities testify even today. However, in modern times such lay groups have received a special stimulus, resulting in the birth and spread of a multiplicity of group forms: associations, groups, communities, movements. We can speak of a new era of group endeavours of the lay faithful. In fact, alongside the traditional forming of associations, and at times coming from their very roots, movements and new sodalities have sprouted, with a specific feature and purpose, so great is the richness and the versatility of resources that the Holy Spirit nourishes in the ecclesial community, and so great is the capacity of initiative and the generosity of our lay people. (CL, 29)

The Holy Father says that "in modern times such lay groups have received a special stimulus." What is the special stimulus in modern times for the Secular Order of Our Lady of Mount Carmel and Saint Teresa of Jesus? I think that the special stimulus is the pastoral problem to which Truman Dickens refers and the responsibility of lay-people to participate in the evangelization of the world. The world has a need of what Carmel has to offer, and Carmel has a responsibility to speak its message to the world. The days of relying on the priest to do everything have long passed, as most of you already know. Every vocation brings a responsibility. Being a Carmelite is not a spiritual pastime; it is a spiritual responsibility.

The third citation (CL, 30) is very important because it expresses clearly what the Church hopes for in the collaboration of lay groups:

> It is always from the perspective of the Church's communion and mission, and not in opposition to the freedom to associate, that one understands the necessity of having clear and definite criteria for discerning and recognizing such lay groups, also called "Criteria of Ecclesiality."
>
> The following basic criteria might be helpful in evaluating an association of the lay faithful in the Church:
>
> - The primacy given to the call of every Christian to holiness, as it is manifested in the fruits of grace which the spirit produces in the faithful and in a growth towards the fullness of Christian life and the perfection of charity. In this sense whatever association of the lay faithful there might be, it is always called to be more of an instrument leading to holiness in the Church, through fostering and promoting a more intimate unity between the everyday life of its members and their faith.

- The responsibility of professing the Catholic faith, embracing and proclaiming the truth about Christ, the Church and humanity, in obedience to the Church's Magisterium, as the Church interprets it. For this reason every association of the lay faithful must be a forum where the faith is proclaimed as well as taught in its total content.

- The witness to a strong and authentic communion in filial relationship to the Pope, in total adherence to the belief that he is the perpetual and visible center of unity of the universal Church, and with the local Bishop, "the visible principle and foundation of unity" in the particular Church, and in "mutual esteem for all forms of the Church's apostolate."

- The communion with Pope and Bishop must be expressed in loyal readiness to embrace the doctrinal teachings and pastoral initiatives of both Pope and Bishop. Moreover, Church communion demands both an acknowledgment of a legitimate plurality of forms in the associations of the lay faithful in the Church and at the same time, a willingness to cooperate in working together.

- Conformity to and participation in the Church's apostolic goals, that is, the evangelization and sanctification of humanity and the Christian formation of people's conscience, so as to enable them to infuse the spirit of the gospel into the various communities and spheres of life. From this perspective, every one of the group forms of the lay faithful is asked to have a missionary zeal which will increase their effectiveness as participants in a re-evangelization.

- A commitment to a presence in human society, which in light of the Church's social doctrine, places it at the service of the total dignity of the person.

> Therefore, associations of the lay faithful must become fruitful outlets for participation and solidarity in bringing about conditions that are more just and loving within society.
>
> The fundamental criteria mentioned at this time find their verification in the actual fruits that various group forms show in their organizational life and the works they perform, such as: the renewed appreciation for prayer, contemplation, liturgical and sacramental life, the reawakening of vocations to Christian marriage, the ministerial priesthood and the consecrated life; a readiness to participate in programs and Church activities at the local, national and international levels; a commitment to catechesis and a capacity for teaching and forming Christians; a desire to be present as Christians in various settings of social life and the creation and awakening of charitable, cultural and spiritual works; the spirit of detachment and evangelical poverty leading to a greater generosity in charity towards all; conversion to the Christian life or the return to Church communion of those baptized members who have fallen away from the faith. (CL, 30)

Apostolate and Service

While we can say that the first three criteria are well in place in the structure of the Secular Order, what needs to be more clearly expressed are the last two criteria. The point of these principles of ecclesiality is not the individual apostolates of members, but the apostolates of the group or the Community. The idea expressed over and over again in *Christifideles Laici* is the participation in evangelization of the group. Before the Council and before the changes in the world and Church that have taken place in the last thirty years, the participation of laypersons in the apostolate of the Church was generally understood as auxiliary to the apostolate exercised by the clergy and religious. With the Council and, above all, with *Christifideles Laici,* the movement of the Holy Spirit is the need for a more concentrated participation of the associations of laypersons in collaboration with the structures of the Church in the evangelization of the world. Applying this principle to Carmel and to the Secular Order of Carmel, there is a need for a greater collaboration in the apostolate of our charism. Every vocation is ecclesial—in and for the good of the whole Church. If you have received the grace of a vocation in Carmel, it is so that you might give what you have received. It is your children, your parents, your brothers and sisters, your neighbors, your coworkers, and your fellow citizens who need what your have received. Again, I repeat, the question is not addressed to you as individuals. The question is addressed to your communities or fraternities: What can WE do as a community of Carmelites to share with the church and the world the spirituality of Saints Teresa of Jesus and Saint John of the Cross?

Accepting the call of the Church expressed in *Christifideles Laici* with the principles of ecclesiality (CL, 30), what does this call ask of the Secular Order of Our Lady of Mount Carmel and Saint Teresa of Jesus?

One by one, how do we express the five principles of ecclesiality in the legislation of the OCDS?

The first of the actual fruits given in number 30 of *Christideles Laici* is "the renewed appreciation for prayer, contemplation, liturgical and sacramental life." How can the communities of the OCDS serve the needs of the Church and world by making these fruits an "actual fruit" of its Carmelite vocation?

As I mentioned at the beginning of this talk, we are not here to discuss the theories of the theology of the layperson in the Church. We are here to discover how to express in our legislation the richness and the responsibility of the charism of those laypersons who have been called to live the spirituality of Saint Teresa of Jesus at the service of the Church. One element of the Teresian Carmelite charism is eremitical. One element is contemplative. One element is service. One element is community. One element is Marian. Please do not profess one or two elements to the exclusion of the other elements. Gilbert Chesterton, and English Catholic commentator, defined a heretic as "one who has a part of the truth and thinks he has the whole truth."

Your vocation is rich. And it is also a responsibility. And you only discover the fullness of its richness by living its responsibility.

The Holy Spirit —Lord and Giver of Life: Carmel and Renewal

The subject that I would like to present for your consideration is taken from the Congress of the Secular Order celebrated in Rome in October 1996. It is expressed in this quote: "The future of the Secular Carmel depends precisely on the active, mature, and responsible collaboration (with the Holy Spirit) in the apostolate of the Order on all levels."

There is a supposition in this subject as it is worded that is fundamental, but which must be stated explicitly. That supposition is that the future of the Order depends precisely on the Order's ability to work in a united way on all levels. You, as men and women, have a vocation to live out your baptismal call to sanctity in allegiance to Jesus Christ, as the rule of Saint Albert says, following the way indicated by Teresa of Jesus. You are not additions to the Order of Discalced Carmelites or auxiliary members of the Order. You are an integral part of the Order.

The Church celebrated a synod in 1995, the subject of which was the religious life. The Holy Father wrote an Apostolic Exhortation, dated March 25, 1996, which was addressed to the whole Church. In that Apostolic Exhortation, entitled *Vita Consecrata*, he spoke about the secular orders associated with religious communities of men and women. He said in number 54. "The laity are therefore invited to share more intensely in the spirituality and mission of these institutes. We may say that, in the light of certain historical experiences such as those of the secular or third orders, a new chapter, rich in hope, has begun in the history of relations between consecrated persons and the laity."

An earlier synod, the Synod on the Laity in 1987, studied the role of the laity in the Church. The document that came from that synod, entitled *Christifideles Laici,* said this (15) about the relationship between religious and laity: "Among the lay faithful this one baptismal dignity takes on a manner of life which sets a person apart without, however, bringing about a separation from the ministerial priesthood or from men and women religious. The Second Vatican Council has described this manner of life as the 'secular character,' the secular character is properly and particularly that of the lay faithful" (LG, 32).

To understand properly the lay faithful's position in the Church in a complete, adequate, and specific manner, it is necessary to come to a deeper theological understanding of their secular character in the light of God's plan of salvation and in the context of the mystery of the Church. Pope Paul VI said, "the Church has an authentic secular dimension, inherent to her inner nature and mission, which is deeply rooted in the mystery of the Word Incarnate and which is realized in different forms through her members" (Address to Members of Secular Institutes, February 2, 1972).

"The new chapter" to which the Pope refers is the new chapter in the history of the Church begun at the Second Vatican Council. It is the chapter that, as we believers recognize in faith, is the direct result of the Holy Spirit's impulse and inspiration in the workings of the Church. The most apparent changes that the Council mandated are perhaps those in the celebration of the liturgy. They were rapid in coming. And they were perhaps the easiest to organize. But the real changes are yet to be seen in some senses. The Church's self-understanding and self-definition is what is most radical. And we only have a glimpse of what those changes are. When the Council used the expression "The People of God" to identify its structure, something new began in our history. It is not incidental that we in the Order stopped using the expressions "first," "second," and "third Orders" to identify ourselves. We are Carmelite friars, Carmelite nuns, and

Carmelite seculars. You are not shadows of the religious who form the real Carmelites. You are real Carmelites. Therefore, the elements of your Carmelite identity ought not to be those elements that are the identifying elements of the religious. The hierarchical structure is essential to the nature of the Church precisely because it identifies the responsibility and area of competence of each of the members of the Order.

In the quote from the Vatican Council, it says that the invitation is to "share more intensely in the spirituality and mission" of the Order. That word "mission" is an extremely important word. We are only beginning to see how it is that the role of the laity in the Church, and therefore the Order, will take shape in the future which it is our responsibility to build. Up until the Council, we were much clearer on the ways in which we shared in the spirituality of the Order than in the mission of the Order. What is becoming more and more obvious in the Church and the Order is the responsibility you have in the area of the apostolate and mission of the Church and the Order.

With this understanding as the background, I want to look at the person of the Holy Spirit, the Lord and Giver of life, the Divine Person who has and always will be the one to give life and renew constantly the life we receive. To the degree that we follow the "impulses of the Holy Spirit," we are always new. If any of us does just what we want to do, because we want to do it, and the Spirit wants us to do something else, we may continue to do it, but it will be fruitless for oneself as well as for others.

Jesus says in the Gospel of John

> "and yet I can say truly that it is better for you I should go away; he who is to befriend you will not come to you unless I do go, but if only I make my way there, I

> will send him to you. He will come, and it will be for him to prove the world wrong, about sin, and about righteousness of heart, and about judging. About sin; they have not found belief in me. About righteousness of heart; I am going back to my Father, and you are not to see me any more. About judging; he who rules this world has had sentence passed on him already. I have still much to say to you, but it is beyond your reach as yet. It will be for him, the truth giving Spirit, when he comes, to guide you in all truth. He will not utter a message on his own; he will utter the message that has been given to him; and he will make plain to you what is still to come. And he will bring honour to me, because it is from me that he will derive what he makes plain to you. I say that he will derive from me what he makes plain to you to you, because all that belongs to the Father belongs to me. (Jn 16: 7–15)

1. The coming of the Holy Spirit depends directly on the mystery of the incarnate Lord.
2. We do not know all that is to be known.
3. The Holy Spirit is the Divine Person who guides us in the truth—but it is a journey made in faith.

We refer to Pentecost as the birthday of the Church. We ask the Holy Spirit to fill our hearts and enlighten our minds. The Holy Spirit is the very air that the Church breathes to keep alive. Jesus, returning to the Father, keeps his promise and sends the Holy Spirit, confirming in that sending of the Spirit, the fundamental mystery of God's self revelation—the Trinity. The Council document on Divine Revelation, *Dei Verbum* (2), says: "In His goodness and wisdom God chose to reveal Himself and to make known to us the hidden purpose of His will (see Eph 1:9) by which through Christ, the Word made flesh, man might in the Holy Spirit have access to the Father and come to share in the divine nature (see Eph 2:1S; 2 Peter 1:4). Through this revelation, therefore, the invisible God (see Col 1:15; 1 Tim 1:17) out of the abundance of His love speaks to men as friends (see Ex 33:11; John 15:14–15) and lives among them (see Bar 3:38), so that He may invite and take them into fellowship with Himself." God, one in three, through the presence of the Spirit reveals Himself as He is on the day of Pentecost, and the Father, the Son, and the Holy Spirit make their dwelling with us. That presence changes humanity.

Saint Luke, in the Acts of the Apostles, also known as the Gospel of the Holy Spirit, describes the change that takes place in the tiny group of believers in the resurrection of Jesus.

> "These occupied themselves continually with the apostle's teaching, their fellowship in the breaking of the bread, and the fixed times of prayer, and every soul was struck with awe, so many were the wonders and signs performed by the apostles in Jerusalem. All the faithful held together and shared all they had, selling their possessions and their means of livelihood, so as to distribute to all, as each had need. They persevered with one accord, day by day, in the temple worship, and as they broke bread in this house or that, took their share of food with gladness and simplicity of heart, praising God, and winning favour with all the people. And each day the Lord added to their fellowship others that were to be saved. (Acts 2, 42–47)

There are then four signs (marks, characteristics) of the transforming presence of the Holy Spirit:

1. Listening to the teaching of the apostles,
2. Fellowship (unity),

3. Breaking of the bread, and
4. Prayer.

These four characteristics, then, were and always will be the productive evidence of the presence of the Holy Spirit in the life of the Church, and what we say of the life of the Church is, of course, true of the life of the Order. Each one of them needs to be understood and given its proper place in the understanding of the Church.

Listening to the teaching of the apostles. What did the apostles teach? It is evident from the writings of the New Testament that what they taught was knowledge of the life of Jesus—his miracles, his attention to the sick, the weak, sinners, his teaching, a new way of understanding the revelation that preceded him in the Old Testament, and an interpretation of the facts of life and history in the light of the good news of God's presence among us. Saint Cyprian said that the Gospel is always much more convincing when it is lived. Cardinal Suenens said that you might be the only Gospel that some people ever read. The teaching of the apostles was that the life, death, and resurrection of Jesus make all the difference in the world.

Fellowship—fraternal union, unity, community. In one sense that might be understood in the light of the sharing of goods referred to in the Acts of the Apostles. But in the first sense, I think it refers to the spiritual union that is the obvious will of Jesus expressed in the 17th chapter of Saint John's Gospel—"that all might be one," a unity based on the truth revealed in the mystery of the life of Jesus.

The breaking of bread. The third element of the Spirit's presence was the breaking of bread, Saint Luke's expression of the celebration of the Eucharist. It was the Eucharist that nourished and strengthened the followers of Christ. The celebration of his presence and his passion motivated them to live the Gospel. Fellowship and breaking of bread go together here in a very intimate union.

Prayer. Intimate relationship with God, praise, supplication, self-knowledge, and contrition. This translation uses the expression of fixed times of prayer, I don't think so much to show some adhesion to a certain horarium, as to be able to facilitate meeting together for the purpose of prayer, and I think the context of the reading supports that interpretation. Everything else is done together. Why should this element be left up to only the individual?

The presence of the Holy Spirit changed the believers in the Lord's resurrection and formed them into the community of believers, the Church. These four elements express the change made in individual believers. These four elements continue to be the expression of the change made in individual believers. These four elements are profoundly Teresian, because the Holy Spirit profoundly moved Teresa. They are, therefore, expressions of the Teresian way of life and the apostolate of the Order.

What I believe to be expressed in the statement that the future of the Secular Carmel depends on the collaboration with the Holy Spirit in the apostolate of the Order is the emphasis on the responsibility that is yours because of the call to live the Carmelite vocation as Seculars. This is the new thing. Again returning to the call of the Holy Father in Vatican Council, intensely share in the spirituality and mission of the Order. That is to say, you are not called nor moved by the Holy Spirit to be simply members of the Order in order to share in the spiritual privileges of your Carmelite identity. You are called to be agents of what Carmel has to offer the world through its spiritual heritage.

What do you have to give? The formation you have received as Carmelite Seculars has been given to you so that you might "actively, maturely, and responsibly collaborate with the Holy Spirit in the apostolate of the Order."

Truman Dickens, in his now famous book on the spirituality of Teresa of Jesus and John of the Cross, *The Crucible of Love,* said that the most pressing pastoral problem of the modern world is to teach people how to pray. The understanding behind the statement on the future of the Secular Carmel is that because of what you receive though your Carmelite vocation, you have the responsibility, but more than that, the capacity to communicate what you receive to others.

Simply look at the four characteristic elements of the presence of the Holy Spirit in the birth of the Church through the experience of your Carmelite vocation in order to see how what you have received has taken fruit in you.

Listening to the apostles' teaching. First of all, listening. The very first thing any of us has to learn in the growth of our spiritual life is the contemplative quality of listening. Only silence produces the quality of listening. We live in a world polluted with noise. I travel public transportation all over the world and am constantly struck by the number of people, both old and young, who constantly have ear-plugs connected to cassette and CD players to accompany them—endless noise. The lessening of the ability to listen affects greatly the capacity to dialogue.

Listening to teaching. Listening to someone else other than you in order to learn. The explosion of information and the demand of our society that you know and the rapidity with which we can know things through such wonderful things like the Internet have also affected the contemplative quality of wonder, of awe. Gone from our society is the mystical wonder of not knowing.

The second element—fellowship is at the heart of Teresian spirituality and our formation as Carmelites. The discipline of forming community, with all the sacrifices it entails, is an art that this world of rugged individualism and fractured relationships needs to relearn. The presence of a community of men and women with a mature spirituality of prayer and relationship with God and each other enriches the local Church.

Breaking of bread. Nearly all, if not all. Saint Teresa's mystical experiences of God took place in the context of the Eucharist—the body of Christ, which she saw as the experience of His most Sacred Humanity. A commitment to living fully the sacramental life of the Church has to lead to a desire to share the richness found in that life with others. The final sections of the post-synod document *Christifideles Laici* speak of the necessity of forming those who can form others.

And, finally, the gift of prayer. What prayer, and the life of prayer, is in our lives because of what we receive through the grace of our formation as Carmelites can only reach its fullness in us when it is productive for others as well. Saint Teresa says in the seventh mansions, the 4th chapter, "O my Sisters! How forgetful this soul, in which the Lord dwells in so particular a way, should be of its own rest, how little it should care for its honor, and how far it should be from wanting esteem in anything! For if it is with Him very much, as is right, it should think little about itself. All its concern is taken up with how to please Him more and how or where it will show Him the love it bears Him. This is the reason for prayer, my daughters, the purpose of this spiritual marriage: the birth always of good works, good works."

The call to holiness is never self-centering. It never has been. Truly holy people have always sought to make God known, that is to say, they have always been evangelizers. Your vocation to Carmel means that you have received a call to holiness precisely so that you might evangelize others. There is an apostolic purpose to your vocation. The signs of the times, the call of history, is expressed in the statement that "the future of the Secular Carmel depends precisely on the active, mature and responsible collaboration (with the Holy Spirit) in the apostolate of the Order on all levels."

I close with another quote from *Vita Consecrata*. It is a quote specifically addressed to religious Orders, but certainly applies to you as well. "You have not only a glorious history to remember and recount, but also a great history still to be accomplished. Look to the future, where the Spirit is sending you in order to do even greater things" (*Vita Consecrata,* 110).

Origin and the Basic Identity of the Secular Order

If a person looks for the history or origin of the Third Orders or Secular Orders and wants to go back to the earliest mention of those Orders, that person finds at the bottom of this search the figure of Saint Francis of Assisi. It was Francis of Assisi who understood, even if only intuitively, that the way to weave the spirituality of his new religious family into the fabric of daily life was through the establishment of an Order of laypersons or diocesan clergy who lived in the world and faced the daily struggles of Christian life. Pope Honorius III approved the first rule for the Franciscan Secular Order in 1221. They were then called "The Brothers and Sisters of Penance."

By presenting the rule to the Pope for approbation, Saint Francis recognized that what he was doing was something "ecclesial," not just something particular to his new Order. This "ecclesial" event is reflected in Canon 312 of the Code of Canon Law, which states that only the Holy See may establish universal or international associations. This authority of the Holy See is delegated to the General of each mendicant Order, and specifically to the General of the Discalced Carmelite Order by Pope Clement VIII in two papal documents, *Cum Dudum,* 23 March 1594, and *Romanum Pontificem*, 20 August 1603.

Certainly, religious life and religious families existed before Saint Francis. Monastic life had flourished in Europe thanks to Saint Benedict. The Benedictines and other forms of monastic life had the institutions of "oblates" for centuries. The identity and structure of oblates has gone through many changes in history. They are, however, always attached to the basic identity of monastic life, that is, identified with one particular monastery for life.

Mendicant life, beginning with Orders such as the Franciscans, Dominicans, Carmelites, etc., had a different structure and purpose. The articles in the *Catholic Encyclopedia* point out the differences that exist in the spirituality and apostolate of monastic life and mendicant Orders. Basically, roughly, and only in the broadest way, one might say that the involvement of laypersons with monastic life was to bring those persons in the world into the spirituality of the monastery, and the involvement of laypersons with mendicant life was to bring the spirituality of the mendicant Orders into the life of laypersons in the world.

The mendicant Orders sought to live a spirituality and exercise an apostolate that grew out of the spirituality that they lived. Many congregations of religious life have existed for a period of time and have gone out of existence because the reason or reasons for their existence ceased. These congregations of religious life based their identity on the specific apostolate for which they were founded. Some active congregations of Sisters today, which have made major contributions to the good of society, are actively seeking a renewed identity because their identity has changed. Some others have decided to stop seeking vocations and to go out of existence, because work by them is no longer necessary. A generation or two ago, Catholic hospitals always had Sisters as a mainstay of the nursing staff.

In any case, mendicant Orders do not base their identity on an apostolate, but on a spirituality, and the spirituality guides and directs the apostolates to which they dedicate themselves. The spirituality of the mendicant Orders reflects elements or an element that belongs to the essence of the Church in the world. The dedication of the Dominicans to higher education is a fruit of Dominican spirituality of the preacher who spreads the word. Much of the Franciscan apostolate is a dedication to working with the poor. This is the fruit of the Franciscan desire to follow Jesus in the purity and simplicity of the

Gospel. Augustinian spirituality is based on a desire to discover Jesus in the midst of community life, which leads them to a dedication to many social apostolates. And the Teresian Carmel's charism is based on the place of the personal relationship between God and the person found in prayer. From that base flows the work to which Carmelites dedicate themselves.

The Secular Order of the mendicant Orders is not just an associated laity. Through the connection to the friars of the different Orders, the Secular Order communicates the spirituality of the Orders to the world around it. It can honestly be said that if the Secular Order did not exist, something would be lacking in the spirituality and presence of the mendicant Orders.

The Secular Order is not conventual nor monastic, but definitely secular; that is, it does not exercise its responsibility in the convent or in the monastery, but in the world *(saeculum)*. The Secular Order is definitely an Order, because of the essential relationship that exists between the friars and the seculars. The relationship between the friars and the seculars is not incidental. It is essential. The Secular Order is a distinct branch of the Order, as the Constitutions indicate. The seculars, however, do not exist as an independent branch of the Order. Distinct, yes. Independent, no. It is for that reason that the Holy See gives the faculty of establishing Secular Order communities to the Superior General of the friars.

There has been a development over the centuries of the role and identity of the Secular Orders, and that includes the Secular Order of the Discalced Carmelites. This development is directly related to the development of the role and identity of laypersons in the Church. Of all the documents I might be able to quote about the role of the Secular Order in the life of the Order, the most concrete and forceful comes from a document directed to the consecrated life, not the laypersons.

"Today, often as a result of new situations, many Institutes have come to the conclusion that their charism can be shared with the laity. The laity are therefore invited to share more intensely in the spirituality and mission of these Institutes. We may say that, in the light of certain historical experiences such as those of the Secular or Third Orders, a new chapter, rich in hope, has begun in the history of relations between consecrated persons and the laity."

I have noted in other places that the new element in this text is the responsibility to "share more intensely in the spirituality and mission." Spirituality was always understood, but mission is new. And it is specifically this directive to the Orders that made necessary a more serious commitment on the part of the Order to the development and formation of the members of the Secular Order. The necessity of the General to have a delegate became more apparent as the Secular Order was growing. Another necessity was that of placing the communities of the Secular Order that were established in places where there are no friars directly under the General Secretariat.

Remembering that the Secular Order is ecclesial and international by its own nature, it was also necessary for the Center of the Order to take a more active role in guiding and developing the formation programs of the OCDS. If a Secular Order member lives the spirituality of the Order and becomes active in the mission of the Order, then the Order better be the one to guide the formation. In a very real sense, the formation of the Secular Order members is subject to approval by the Center of the Order. Formation is not the private project of a particular community or even of a Province. Formation is the responsibility of the Order.

Within the bounds of the relationship between the friars and the seculars, the seculars certainly have their autonomy. In the Discalced Carmelite Order, that autonomy has always been expressed in the various rules that existed before the Manual, in the Manual of 1922, in the Rule of Life on 1979, and in the current legislation of the Constitutions. The autonomy touches upon matters of formation, leadership, and governance.

In summary, Saint Francis of Assisi, who initiated the idea of establishing an Order of laypersons identifiably part of the Order, and the Church, through the approbation of Honorius III, recognized that the Secular Order was indeed ecclesial. The current legislation of the Church in the Code of Canon Law, as well as the current legislation of the Secular Order of the Discalced Carmelites, recognizes the relationship that exists between the friars and the seculars. The Order as a whole, friars and seculars, have a responsibility to work together, especially in the area of formation of the members so that they might represent to the world in which they live the spirit and mission of Carmel. The responsibility of the Center of the Order is to ensure and guide the development of the adequate formation of the members of the Secular Order.

The Beatitudes and Your Vocation to Carmel

You have made the Promise

I am not really good at giving very theoretical conferences. I would rather be as practical as I can possibly be and talk about the things that have to do with your vocation and my responsibility in regard to your vocation.

I think that the Promise is the most neglected part of formation programs that I have seen. There are many different religious orders. There are Franciscans, Dominicans, Oblates, Missionaries of Mary Immaculate, and the Jesuits; there are all sorts of different religious traditions and religious families, but what makes the friars, or the priests, or the brothers, and the nuns and sisters and what makes us religious are that we make vows. I am a priest because I was ordained, not because I am a Carmelite. I was professed and the Church recognized in my profession my dedication of myself as a religious and as a Carmelite.

What makes you a member of the Secular Order is that you have made the Promise. It is your Promise that makes you a member of the Secular Order. Your Promise distinguishes you from many, many, many other people who live and love Carmelite spirituality but have not made any sort of commitment to the Order and whose commitment has not been recognized by the Church. What makes you a member of Secular Order of Discalced Carmelites is not that you live Carmelite spirituality, because there are a lot of other people who may even live it better than all of us put together, who are not members of the Order. What makes you a member of the Secular Order is that you have made the Promise. Your Promise has been recognized by the Church. There are a lot of other people who are part of the Carmelite family who are not part of the Order. There are a lot of people who know a lot of things about Carmelite spirituality and really are experts but are not members of the Order.

How does this come up in a practical way? Let me give an example. I bet in some of your Communities you have the experience of people who got through the entire formation program, make Definitive Promises, may even make vows, and then you never see them again. If you do see them…" well I say my office every day, I make mental prayer every day, I read Saint Teresa, I read Saint John of the Cross, I study them," but they have no idea of what it means to be a part of the Order. I am asked that question. I know that is the truth because, no matter where I go in the world, somebody asks me about people who made the Promise and then never come to meetings again. I have asked to look at many formation programs and most formation programs have zero in it about making or what the Promise is, the content of the Promise.

What it means to become part of a community

Why is there a Promise? What is the effect of making the Promise? It is almost like I want to say that there is too much formation in spirituality in the initial stages and not enough formation in what it means to become part of a Community, because it is the Promise that incorporates you into the Order. So, I have a chance because I have been asked to talk about the Beatitudes, the Beatitudes in not just a Bible study program. It is incorporation; it is part of your commitment to incorporate yourself to become part of this family. The friars, the nuns, we live in community, it is our structure. Your structure is to make community. You don't live in community, you live in the community of your families, you live in the community of your parishes, but you make a Community of the people who share something very basic, about your Catholic Christian identity, namely, Carmel.

In order to put the Beatitudes in the context of the Promise, I want to read in the new Constitutions what it says about the following of Jesus in the Teresian Carmel, because that is where it talks about the Promise. It does not talk about prayer. The third chapter talks about prayer. The second chapter talks about incorporation. It does not talk about spirituality and the formation for spirituality or rather the information for spirituality. That is the fourth chapter. The first chapter is identity, values, and commitment, which leads to the second chapter, which is following Jesus in the Teresian Secular Carmel and that has to do with the Promise. It is how you follow Jesus. Let me read a few of the numbers in the Constitution.

Constitution number 10: Christ is the center of our lives and of Christian experience. Members of the Secular Order are called to live the demands of following Christ in union with Him, by accepting His teachings and devoting themselves to Him. To follow Jesus is to take part in His saving mission of proclaiming the Good News and the establishment of God's Kingdom. There are various ways of following Jesus: all Christians must follow Him, must make Him the law for their lives and be disposed to fulfill three fundamental demands: to place family ties beneath the interests of the Kingdom and Jesus himself; to live in detachment from wealth in order to show that the arrival of the Kingdom does not depend on human means but rather on God's strength and the willingness of the human person before Him; to carry the cross of accepting God's will revealed in the mission that He has confided to each person.

Constitution number 11: Following Jesus as members of the Secular Order is expressed by the Promise to strive for evangelical perfection in the spirit of the evangelical counsels of chastity, poverty and obedience and through the beatitudes. By means of this Promise the member's baptismal commitment is strengthened for the service of God's plan in the world. This Promise is a pledge to pursue personal holiness, which necessarily carries with it a commitment to serving the Church in faithfulness to the Teresian Carmelite charism. The Promise is taken before the members of the community, representing the whole Church and in the presence of the Delegate of the Superior of the Order. By the Promise made to the community in the presence of the Superior of the Order or his Delegate, the person becomes a full member of the Secular Order.

So the Promise, but the parts of the Promise, that is the fact of the act of committing yourself. It is not just personal, as it says in other parts of the Constitution; it is ecclesial. Your promise is an ecclesial act. You are more part of the Church, because you are a member of the Order. The essential element, the element that distinguishes, as I have already said, every other person who follows Carmelite spirituality is that you make a commitment to the Order and the Order makes a commitment to you.

That commitment is recognized by the Church. For that reason it is not just a club. Many people have a club mentality about the Secular Order; that's why they stop coming, or they come when it is convenient or they come when it is almost time for elections. I can always tell that there are some things that are universal truths.

People generally admit that they know somebody who does that. Club membership can hardly be the correct mentality for forming a community with people. That mentality that says I come when I come when it is convenient for me, that mentality that says I come so that I can learn all this and do it for myself: that I say the office, I read it myself, I say my prayers, I meditate every day, and I might even meditate an hour and a half or two hours every day. I might read and know all about Saint Teresa and Saint John of the Cross.

One of the things that is in the Constitutions when it talks about Provincial Councils and Provincial Statutes, the first thing that Provincial Statutes are to do is to develop an adequate program of formation. Not just a program of information: most of the time when people say we need a program of formation, they are talking about a program of information. We want to know what to teach in this period, in this period, this period, this period, and this period. What books to use in this stage, and this stage, and this stage. That is not formation; that is a program of information. Formation is much more than information. Good formation depends on good information, that's true. If you get bad information, you have bad formation. Formation is much more than just information. Information is what; formation is how. So a program of formation is, How do we train people, and how do we educate people? How do we inform people so that they make progress in the stages of formation and can commit themselves to us?

The Promise is made to the Community into which the person is incorporated. So the formation of the person is to be able to commit himself or herself to us with the right information. I have seen so many programs of information for formation programs, a lot of spirituality but not a lot of corporality—you might say incorporation. Remember what Saint Teresa says? That is useless or it is silly to think of ourselves as angels as long as we have these bodies. The Secular Order is an extension of the Church. It is a realization of the Church, which is, by nature, incarnate. It has a body and soul. The soul is the spirituality, but it gives life to a body which is the incorporation of people with each other. Many times this is the reason why people have been satisfied with learning a lot about spirituality but, not being able to incorporate it, cease to participate, because they do not see the necessity.

The Promise is as the Constitution is saying: to strive for evangelical perfection in the spirit of the evangelical counsels of chastity, poverty, and obedience and through the Beatitudes. The evangelical counsels are traditional and are, of course, what the friars, the sisters, the nuns, and religious make in their vows as they incorporate themselves into the Community in which they are members. The evangelical counsels are time honored, long standing. It defines a way of living Christ's life. Poverty, chastity, obedience or whatever order you want to put them in, chastity, obedience, poverty, those vows, those counsels, they are evangelical counsels.

As you know there are many people; especially after the Second Vatican Council, there was in the Church and in the Order also a movement to really make the Secular Order independent of the friars and nuns in the sense of having their own forms, forms that are different from our forms. There was a movement, after the Second Vatican Council, that wanted to de-religousize the religioused and de-religiousize the Secular Order. They wanted to take away even poverty, chastity, and obedience and say there has to be something else. In every group, in order for a group to function, to survive, to have history, and to continue in history, it is necessary to have three things: discernment of who is part of the group, formation of the people who are discerned to belong as part of the group, and the commitment for the purposes of the groups. Commitment is necessary.

Poverty, Chastity, and Obedience

As time went along and different people were trying to come up with different things, we realized that poverty, chastity, and obedience are evangelical counsels. They are not counsels to religious. They are evangelical counsels. They are ways of evaluating yourself in the light of Jesus. Because the vows we make as religious and the

Promise you make as seculars are not to live our poverty, our chastity, our obedience, but to live the poverty and the chastity and the obedience of Jesus. My chastity is not going to save anybody, but it is the poverty and the chastity and the obedience of Jesus that saves. So we live Jesus, that person, second person of the blessed Trinity, God and man, who lived his life on earth and in that life saved all of humanity, whose life is found in the pages of the Gospel and in the experience of the tradition of the Church and in the sacraments and prayer and meditation. That person becomes the standard by which we evaluate ourselves, under those three rather radical categories of human life. Loving, possessing, and being in obedience: how we are. In a certain sense it is that poverty, that chastity, and that obedience of Jesus that in our Promise, in my vows, in your Promise that we make that become the standard for us to evaluate our lives. How we are living, how we are moving, how we are being, how we possess things. We possess things, but how do we possess them? We love, and we love deeply and humanly, but with what clarity do we love? We are and we are incorporated with each other; we are parts of community, parts of family, parts of society, parts of the Church, but how?

At the time of The Rule of Life in 1974, when The Rule of Life was written, the commission that was set up to evaluate the Rule of Life wanted to add something, inspired basically by the Vatican Council's document on the laity, *Apostolicam Actuositatum,* and added as an integral part of the Promise to the personal evaluation of Jesus as the standard of personal life: they wanted to add the Beatitudes. They wanted to add the Beatitudes for a very specific reason because the Beatitudes are not just a personal evaluation of one's own person; of one's own approach, attitude, and living of life; but they are a measure of relationship to the world.

The Beatitudes

What does the Catechism of the Catholic Church say about the Beatitudes? There are two numbers in the Catechism, number 1716 and 1717.

1716 : "The Beatitudes are at the heart of Jesus' preaching. They take up the promises made to the chosen people since Abraham. The Beatitudes fulfill the promises by ordering them no longer merely to the possession of a territory but to the kingdom of Heaven."

1717: "The Beatitudes depict the countenance of Jesus Christ and portray His charity. They express the vocation of the faithful associated with the glory of His passion and resurrection. They shed light on the actions and attitudes characteristic of the Christian life. They are paradoxical promises that sustain hope in the midst of tribulations. They proclaim the blessings and rewards already secured however dimly for Christ's disciples. They have begun in the lives of Virgin Mary and all the saints."

The Beatitudes depict the countenance of Jesus Christ and portray His charity. They express the vocation of the faithful associated with the glory of His passion.

Remember this is a result of the Second Vatican Council document *Apostolicam Actuositatem* which then becomes even more highlighted and underlined and enhanced in the document *Christifideles Laici* on the role of the apostolate of laypersons. It is essential, your role. It is not just because there are less vocations that your role is more important than before. It is because it is the time where the Holy Spirit wants this role. The Church doesn't need friars, the Church doesn't need nuns, and the Church doesn't need seculars.

The Church needs what we have to offer. The Church needs the witness of Saint Teresa and Saint John of the Cross. The Church needs that spirituality. The world needs that spirituality. The world needs what we have to offer; to the extent that we do not offer it, we are useless to God. We are useless to God to the extent that we do not offer what He has given us in our vocation. This commitment that we have made, you through the Promise, I through the vows, is to be present in the Church, to minister to the Church, and this is the role specifically underlined, revealed most in the Second Vatican Council and after the Second Vatican Council through the different Synods about the role of laypersons in the Church. *Vita Apostolica* and *Vita Consecrata* are documents centered on the religious life. Paragraph 55 says that because of the new circumstances in the history of the world, it has become apparent that laypeople are called to share not only the spirituality but the mission….not just spirituality but the mission of the religious family.

The Church needs to know what Saint Teresa and Saint John of the Cross say, and it's our job to tell them, to let them know. There are 40,000 of you. There are 4,000 of us. You are ten times more present than we are. We have to read the Beatitudes as a way to remind us of how our relationship to the world as Communities is. We Americans have a big problem in that we are always tempted to be individualists. We are tempted to always think, "what does this mean I have to do?" Begin to think now as Communities. What does this mean for our Community as a Secular Order Community? Not what does this mean for me. Nobody has to quit their job or leave their families to become a Carmelite Secular if they consider thinking in terms of our Community.

Let's read the Beatitudes. There are two sets of beatitudes. Correct? Not just Matthew, but also Luke.

Saint Matthew's version: 5:1–12

1. Seeing the crowds, he went onto the mountain, and when he was seated, his disciples came to him.
2. Then he began to speak, and this is what he taught them.
3. Blessed are the poor in spirit, the kingdom of heaven is theirs.
4. Blessed are the gentle, they shall have the earth as an inheritance.
5. Blessed are those who mourn, they shall be comforted.
6. Blessed are those who hunger and thirst for uprightness (justice)....
7. Blessed are the merciful, they shall have mercy shown them.
8. Blessed are the pure in heart, they shall see God.
9. Blessed are the peacemakers, they shall be recognized as children of God.
10. Blessed are those who are persecuted in the cause of uprightness (justice), for the kingdom of heaven is theirs.
11. Blessed are you when people abuse you, persecute you, and speak all kinds calumny against you falsely on my account.
12. Rejoice and be glad for your reward will be great in heaven, for this is how they persecuted the prophets before you.

Saint Luke's version: 6:20–26

20. Then fixing his eyes on his disciples, he said: "How blessed are you who are poor, the kingdom of God is yours.
21. Blessed are you who are hungry now, you shall

> have your fill. Blessed are you who are weeping now, you shall laugh.
> 22. Blessed are you when people hate you, drive you out, abuse you, denounce your name as criminal on account of the Son of Man.
> 23. Rejoice when that day comes, and dance for joy, look, your reward will be great in heaven. This was the way their ancestors treated the prophets.
> 24. But woe to you who are rich, for you have your consolation now.
> 25. Woe to you who have plenty to eat now, for you shall go hungry. Woe to those who are laughing now, you shall mourn and weep.
> 26. Woe to you when all speak well of you, this is the way their ancestors treated the false prophets.

Again, as poverty, chastity, and obedience were the measuring stick, were the life of Jesus—Jesus was poor, chaste, and obedient in the Gospel, in his life, in the tradition of the Church—that person then becomes the measuring stick of our own relationship to the Father, especially. The Beatitudes become the measuring stick for where we identify ourselves as our Communities. Because when we do this in Communities, this is again part of that incorporation.

When we do this in Community, we support each other doing it.

We are not left to wondering how or all on our own. But where do we identify ourselves? With whom do we identify ourselves? Because in the Beatitudes, as everybody, you can read many things and commentaries of the Beatitudes to understand that they are the introduction to the Sermon on the Mount, and Jesus and the Sermon on Plain in Luke. The Sermon on the Mount is very much about the relationship of one to another, including of course to pray the Our Father.

How do we identify ourselves as persons who live a life of allegiance to Jesus Christ? This Carmelite life? The Rule of Saint Albert? A life of allegiance to Jesus Christ and that allegiance to Jesus Christ brings us to identify ourselves with certain people and to see in certain aspects and certain virtues and certain approaches to living how we have to live in order to be in allegiance to Jesus Christ, in order to be loyal to Jesus. The structure of the eight Beatitudes that are more famous from the fifth chapter of St. Matthew's Gospel, which you see sometimes hanging on walls, you can see it when you go to religious gift shops and see a plaque that has the eight Beatitudes. People look at them like they belong on a Hallmark card, you know, but they are really very demanding and they are not so cute. They are cute on the card, but they are not so cute in living them out because they are demanding an attitude of us. That doesn't come naturally to us in certain ways. I do not think that it comes naturally to us as Americans—to live the Beatitudes the way the Gospels teach the Beatitudes. And they certainly don't come naturally to us as an approach to living life.

Of the eight Beatitudes, you can almost divide them into two sections of four. I am going to read the traditional ones that I remember from grade school.

> 1. Blessed are the poor in spirit, the kingdom of heaven is theirs.
> 2. Blessed are those who mourn, for they shall be comforted
> 3. Blessed are the meek, for they shall inherit the earth.
> 4. Blessed are you who hunger and thirst for justice, you shall have your fill.

5. Blessed are the merciful, for they will be shown mercy.
6. Blessed are the pure in heart, for they shall see God.
7. Blessed are the peacemakers, for they shall be called children of God.
8. Blessed are those who are persecuted for justice, for the kingdom of heaven is theirs.

Justice

There are two sets. The fourth one and eighth one go together, almost as a refrain, the way we do sometimes in the Psalm response. Blessed are those who hunger and thirst for justice, for they shall have their fill. Blessed are those who are persecuted for justice, for they shall have their fill. The justice that exists in the Bible is not the justice that you and I understood when we say justice is going to be done. We mean justice as punishment. We mean justice as revenge. That is not at all evangelical. That is not at all scriptural. It is not at all the justice of God. I often wonder especially when I am reading the Gospels; it sort of shocks me sometimes, as the day of the Lord is when we let everybody out of prison. We find so many reasons to keep people in prison, because justice has to be done.

We are very conditioned in our attitudes; we get a lot more information about how to live from the television, from the newspaper, the means of communication, than we do from the Gospels. So, we have a tendency to skip over what these things say to us because they are conditioned by how we understand. Blessed are those that hunger and thirst for justice. It is almost like we might exaggeratingly say we understand these as vigilante groups who go out to punish people. They are doing justice. They are not seeking forgiveness.

• Justice is to look out for the poor.
• Justice is to make sure people eat.
• Justice is to make sure people are clothed.
• Justice is to make sure people have what they need to be human and to live humanly.
• Justice is to forgive. One Sister said, "Actions speak louder than words. God's justice was God's mercy."

Through all of tradition so many things, all Christian tradition, in theology, in philosophy, so many other things have interrupted almost, or infused themselves, or inched their way into spirituality, into Scripture, into following Christ that we almost get political in the way we interpret or understand our approach to life, to living. It comes from whom we identify with. One of the things about the American system of justice is that we have the death penalty. Yet the Holy Father so strongly speaks against the death penalty. And, at least according to surveys, a majority of Catholics are in favor of the death penalty.

So our American idea of justice is more important than Jesus' idea of justice. Again, I'm trying to be practical in pointing out that this is not easy, to live an evangelical life. Yet it is what you Promised to do, and that is so solemn, that Promise, that the Church says that's how you become a member. You can quote Saint Teresa up and down, Saint John of Cross left to right, Saint Thérèse, everything, but if you do not follow Jesus, you are not a Carmelite.

Some of us did not know the commitment that God was going to ask of us. As we read the documents of the Church, for that reason we are fortunate in the United States. We have all the footnotes. Read the footnotes to the Constitution, they explain why in the words of the Holy Father, the Pope, in the words of our Holy Father Saint John of the Cross and the words of Saint Teresa, in the words of laws of the Church, the canon law, and explain why. The Beatitudes in the context of the Promise and the Promise in the context of your vocation are the pledge to do what God wants done.

In a nutshell, people, basically what is Carmelite spirituality? Carmelite spirituality is to know God, so that God may be known. Not to just know God. God has his reasons for wanting us to know him, for wanting us to have this relationship with him. The Beatitudes, in a most concrete way, drive us, to show us, where it is that we must show God, the poor, the meek, the mourning, those who suffer. That's where God wants us to be.

The Role of Study in the Secular Order of Discalced Carmelites

Recently, I have been asked about the role of study in the Secular Order of Carmel. Some think that too much emphasis on studying may have the effect of scaring people away from the OCDS. Others think that an emphasis on studying makes the Formation Director's job much more complicated and/or difficult. And others say that there is difficulty in finding adequate Formation Personnel because they are not academically trained to be teachers.

As far as I can, I would like to clarify some issues in regard to study and the OCDS.

The first thing to say is that most of us have an image associated with the word "study" that comes from our own personal experience. When we were in primary school, we had "to study" in order to advance from grade to grade each year. "Study" meant memorizing, practicing, testing, afternoons or evenings in front of books (with our minds sometimes wanting us to be elsewhere). "Study" was competitive. Scores were given and prizes awarded to the ones whose "study" produced the best scores. As we progressed in school and advanced from grade to grade, the "studying" got more and more complicated and, above all, harder. Some people seemed to breeze through. Others succeeded, but at what headaches! But the good thing was, it had an end!

When or if we got to the advanced stages of "study" at university levels or postgraduate levels, we ran into an even finer "study." People in higher degree programs entered into fields of "study" in order to dedicate their lives and energies to "study" one certain thing. They produced the fruit of their academic work in a thesis that sometimes had the title of "The Study of…."

So "study" has, for many of us, an image of "get it over with so you can get out of school" or "dedicate all your energy and time to this one thing."

Neither one of those ideas has anything to do with what the word "study" means in the initial or ongoing formation of the members of the Secular Order. So, to try to understand what "study" is in the life of the secular, please take those ideas and images that you have and put them aside.

First, study in formation of the OCDS is not reduced to some sort of academic pursuit of knowledge that is externally discernable by testing like a mathematical times table.

Second, study in formation of the OCDS is not the sole pursuit of one person to conquer a body of knowledge.

Third, study in formation of the OCDS does not have a point at which one says "The End."

A basic definition of what "study in formation of the OCDS" could be, is the process whereby, with the help of others, we attempt to deepen our understanding of the relationship with God in the light of Catholic and Carmelite doctrine.

Is there a place of academic and intellectual pursuit? Certainly, for those who have the time and the ability and the talent, yes, there is a place. But that is not what all of us need to do in order to "study" our spirituality.

A primary point is that we are all, at all times, in formation. No matter when we made our definitive commitment to the Lord in Carmel, we are still all in formation.

A second point, all of us are helped and accompanied by others in this process of deepening our understanding, be it by a designated person in certain stages or by the Community which serves as support in the relationship with God.

Academic study has a product. Formation study is a process.

Because someone can quote chapter and verse of Saint Teresa, Saint John of the Cross, or Saint Thérèse, does not necessarily mean they have been formed. I have heard the lament: "Our poor Holy Parents (Teresa and John), so often quoted, so little followed!"

There are challenges in this type of study. Not the academic ones…there are no tests, gold stars, blue ribbons.

The challenges are first the desire to deepen the understanding of the relationship with God. That can be very demanding…in fact, it is a lot easier to memorize Saint Teresa.

The second challenge is that you need others to help you, and you need to help others. Also, not so easy.

The third challenge is that it is based on Catholic and Carmelite teaching, not just on the way I think about it all.

So, I hope this helps to see the difference between the "study" that got you through school and the "study" that gets you through life.

How Ought the Council Function?

It would be almost universal to say that if the Council functions as the Council ought to function, the Community will probably function as a Community ought to function. If the Council does not function as the Council ought to function, the Community will definitely not function as the Community ought to function. Many times the divisions that exist in Communities come from Councils that are divided, especially if the Council has on it a perpetual member.

One of the advantages I have is that I don't know anybody or anybody's Community, so I can come in and say things that nobody else can say. I am trying to say what sometimes are the roots of divisions that exist in Communities, and why the Community does not reflect or have the ability to live that experience is because as a Community there are division that exist because this person was not elected. They were not elected as President and they are on the Council and they are upset, because they really wanted to be President. They set up sort of unconsciously many times a copresidency; or an antipresidency. There is a division in the community. Or it comes time for the Council to vote on people, and somebody says something against somebody or a negative opinion about something and one of the people on the Council goes out and tells the person. It happens, I think, where people say things that are said in the Council. Then the Council stops functioning as a Council because the person who is spoken about, her feelings get hurt, then her friends side with her, and it leads to silly division, because the Council did not function as a Council.

The Council has to function as a Council as long as there is respect for what is said in the Council. What do they call that? "Confidentiality." Confidentially, the persons or members of the Council have to be able to speak their mind clearly. They need to understand that it is the way the Holy Spirit works and that it is according to the Constitutions. In Chapter VII of the Constitutions (it's the chapter on Organization and Government), there is a description in there in constitutional terms of the relationship between the friars, nuns, and the seculars, a description of the working relationship between the friars and/or the Spiritual Assistant (if the Spiritual Assistant is not a friar) and the Community ,and somewhat of a description of how the Community ought to function. Remember that we come from a long history of the Secular Order, and I'm sure many of you who have been around the Secular Order for a long time are familiar that at a certain time the term "President" of the Community that we use now, which we've used since the introduction of the Rule of Life, the President of the Community (before the Rule of Life) was referred to as Prior or Prioress (formerly in the Manual). Even though we have changed the term, we haven't always changed the mentality of the approach of understanding how the President should function.

There are numbers in the Constitutions that I will make reference to as we look at the relationship between the friars and the Secular Order and the functioning of the Council.

No. 40. The Secular Order is basically structured on the local Community as a visible sign of the Church. The Community is a visible sign of the Church and that is the basic structure.

No. 43. The Provincial Superior, usually aided by the Provincial Delegate, is the superior of the Secular Order within his territory. He is responsible for the well-being of the Secular Order within the territory of his jurisdiction. He is to make visitations of the Communities in his jurisdiction and after consultation with the Council [of the community] appoint a Spiritual Assistant for Communities. In all cases of disputes, appeal will be made in the first instance to the Provincial.

No. 44. The Spiritual Assistant to each community is usually a friar of the Order. His duty is to give spiritual aid to the Community (not individuals), so that its members may be guided in their vocation and may correspond with it as perfectly as possible. He will also endeavor to promote solidarity between the Secular Community and the friars and nuns of the Order. At the invitation of the Council, he may attend meetings of the Council, without the right to vote. At the different stages of the formation of the candidates, he will be available to interview them. The Council may consult him about the suitability of the candidate to assume the responsibility of the vocation to the Secular Order. He will support the formation of the Community by his availability to the Director of Formation.

However, he may not be the Director of Formation. The Spiritual Assistant must be well-versed in Carmelite spirituality and well-informed in the Church's teaching concerning the role of laypeople in the Church.

No. 46. The Council, composed of the President and three Councilors and the Director of Formation, constitutes the immediate authority of the Community. Who is the superior of the Community? The Council, not the President, not the Formation Director, not the Spiritual Assistant. It is the Council. This is not new. This was in the Rule of Life. And the next sentence in the Constitutions is lifted right out of the Rule of Life. The primary responsibility of the Council is the formation and Christian and Carmelite maturing of the members of the community. The Council is responsible—not the President, not any one Councilor, not the expresident— and not the foundress of the Community.

No. 47. The Council has the authority:

a) to admit candidates to formation, the Promises, and the vows;

b) to reduce, for adequate reasons, the period of formation before temporary Promises, with the permission of the Provincial;

c) to convene the Community for the triennial elections;

d) to replace, for a serious reason, a member of the Council itself;

e) to dismiss a member of the Community, should this be necessary after consulting with the Provincial;

f) to receive a member transferring from another Community; and

g) if a matter should arise that is outside the competence of the Council, it is the obligation of the President to bring it to the attention of the Provincial.

No. 48. The General Superior, the Provincial Superior, and the Council of the Community are the legitimate superiors of the Secular Order.

No. 51. The President, elected from among those who have made Final Promises, has the duty to convoke and preside over the meetings of the Community. He should show fraternal service to all the members of the Community; foster a spirit of Christian and Carmelite affability, being careful to avoid any demonstration of preference for some members over others; coordinate contacts with those members of the Community who because of age, illness, distance or other reasons, are not able to attend meetings; aAid the Director of Formation and Spiritual Assistant in carrying out their responsibilities; in their absence, but only temporarily, he may take their place or designate another to do so from among those who have made Definitive Promises.

No. 52. The responsibility of the three Councilors is to form, with the President, the government of the Community and to support the Director of Formation. Generally, they are Community members with definitive promises. In particular circumstances, members with First Promises can serve as Councilors.

Those numbers, 40, 43, 44, 46, 47, 48, 51, and 52, describe, in constitutional terms, the relationship between the friars (the friars have a role and an obligation to the Seculars). Those numbers also describe the responsibility of the Seculars to take charge of their part of the Order. It bears repeating over and over again, that the Council is the superior of the Community and any one member who speaks, who is a member of the Council, speaks for the Council. But that person can only speak for the Council if that person speaks what the Council thinks. The President doesn't speak and then say to the Council, "this is what we are doing." That's not functioning as a Council; it's not working that way.

President

The superior of the Community is the Council, not the President. The President is not superior of the Community. The President is not even superior of the Council. The President is the spokesperson of the Council, the mouthpiece. Some mouthpieces are very mouthy. The President speaks for the Council. It is the Council that decides. If you have three councilors who say "yes, ma'am" to the President, you don't have a Council. The Council discusses—the President, the three Councilors, the Formation Director. Those five people make up the Council, who discuss for the good of the Community. The President primarily is the spokesperson for the authority of the Community which is the Council. Now, again, we have come from this tradition where we have had this Prior/Prioress mentality, that the person who was the President was the superior of the Community. As a matter of fact, I have had many experiences of being asked (and remember in 1974 when the Rule of Life was issued and finally approved in 1979 and this structure was present in the Rule of Life, that the Council is the superior of the Community), Who is the superior of the community?, and being answered with "the President," and this is after thirty years. It takes a long time for us to understand change and to put change into practice. Now sometimes it is true because some presidents have acted as superiors of the Community. And sometimes it is true that expresidents act as superior of the Community. I don't know if that is true or not true of your Communities, but I suspect it is true in some places because this happens. It happens in monasteries of nuns, it happens in provinces of friars and it happens in Communities of the Secular Order, where people who had authority don't let go of authority. They understand authority as control of the Community and not as service of the Community.

Council

The Council meets frequently and always and always when necessary in reference to taking care of formation programs and the growth of their own community. I think the Rule of Life said the Council is to meet once a year. That seems awfully minimal if the Council is going to function as a good Council. If the primary responsibility of the Council is the formation and Christian Carmelite maturing of the members, meeting once a year will not help them to be responsible. No one person is responsible for this. The Council is responsible for the formation and the Christian and Carmelite maturing of the members.

So if there are decisions that have to be made in the name of the Council, the Council has to meet in order to arrive at that decision. The Council must meet and discuss, and when the President speaks, the President speaks in the name of the Council, not for the Council and I make a distinction here: I (the President) am going to speak for them and afterward tell them (the Council) what I said. I (the President) am going to speak in their place. But if I (the President) speak in their name, then I speak what our (the council's) decision has been. When I was Provincial, I had three different Councillors, and hopefully, in our Province, when we decided things we decided things in the council by voting on things. And sometimes the vote was 5 to 0 and sometimes the vote was 1 to 4 and I was the 1. But the decision was always announced that "this is what the Council has decided."

It happens sometimes that people (Councillors) are afraid to speak at a Council meeting. The reason they are afraid to speak at a Council meeting is because they are somehow going to be punished by what they think. How are they going to be punished by saying what they think? Because it is going to be repeated. Anybody who is capable (we are all capable) of repeating what is said in Council meetings in order to divide the Community should not be a Council member. They don't have the necessary qualities for being a Council member because they are not there for service to the Community. And that prevents the Council from being able to speak. It prevents the Council from being able to function.

A Council member is always free to talk to another council member or the President about something, but if they think a decision must be made with regard to a certain issue in the name of the Community, which is the Council's responsibility, then the President is obliged to call a meeting of the Council to discuss it. Remember, no one thing has to be decided by the end of each meeting. You can continue to discuss it at another time; maybe you need time to look at the Constitutions in regard to the issue and to think about things before arriving at a decision. It's better to arrive at a good decision late than a bad decision on time. It is the responsibility of the President to convoke and preside over the meetings of the Council. It is the responsibility of the Delegate when making visitations to the Community to see how the Council is functioning and to correct the President if the President says well they are going to arrive at a decision I don't agree with. The President is not the boss. It is important for you to study the whole structure that is in the Constitution. It is the responsibility of the Delegate, when visiting Communities, to pay attention to how the Council is functioning. If we can make sure that the Council is functioning as a Council, we are doing our job of forming the Community, because everything else falls in line if the Council functions properly. Both the Councillors and the Community feel themselves to be a part of the Community, that they are not under the dominance of one person. If the Council members feel that way, the Community feels much more that way. If the President is not there, then the Formation Director can call a Council meeting.

The Provincial Superior usually aided by the Provincial Delegate is the Superior of the Secular Order within his territory, responsible for the well being of the Secular Order. He is to make visitation to the community. When the Provincial through his Delegate makes visitations, he has certain canonical responsibilities and abilities to decide things. One of the things I suggest when I speak to the friars, especially the Provincial Delegates, is for the formation of the Communities as Communities concentrating specifically on the formation of the leaders and the formation people and the Council. If the Council begins to function with this kind of flexibility, then it is the most capable person who becomes a rotating superior or member of the council, changing, then the Community begins to form itself as a Community not just a collection of individuals because what happens when the Council is fractured, when it's three against two against three or five all-person shows. Then everyone in Community just becomes an individual, and the Community doesn't function.

Spiritual Assistant

The relationship that then exists between the friars and the (nuns) and the Secular Order is then this flexible one of service and support. We (the friars) are not always clear on how we are working this out, but we are working this out. And you have to be clear too. Your councils have to be able to take this responsibility, and for this to happen, there has to be communication among the council members. It is true that the Spiritual Assistant can help, but it is a mistake for you to look to the Spiritual Assistant to give you the answer. He can help, guide, support, he may be able to correct certain things, but if you always have him give the answer to your questions, you will not function as a Council. You will be five dependent people, members of the Secular Order, sometimes dependent on someone who is not even a Carmelite. This is not talking about spirituality, this is talking about governance and organization. This is a Carmelite organization. One of the main reasons why we had to redefine the role of Spiritual Assistant is because we were very close to having at least half of the Secular Order communities in the world having someone who is not a Carmelite for a Spiritual Assistant because of the way the Secular Order is growing in places around the world where there are no Carmelite friars. That's why it says the Spiritual Assistant is usually a friar of the Order. So we can't have the structure depending on some-one who is not a member of the Order. In the Ritual it spoke of the Spiritual Assistant as a representative of the Order. And that is all well and good in Italy or Spain where practically all of the Secular Order communities meet in the monastery of the friars where the friar can roll out of bed and into the meeting. For many of your communities to have a friar come, he has to take a plane to get there or drive for a long time or, in the Philippines, take a boat ride for hours to get from one place to another to attend a meeting. The Spiritual Assistant cannot be the depending point for your function as a Council. What I am trying to describe is how the Council should function, the type of people who should be on the Council, and how important confidentiality is for the Council to function.

Many times Councils were very dependent on the decisions or opinions made by the Spiritual Assistant. It's not the Spiritual Assistant's community. It's your community. If I'm the assistant, you can ask me anything and I am not afraid to give my opinion. If you don't ask me, I have no right to give it. I have a right to give it in my community to which I belong as a Carmelite, which is the friars. That's where I have the obligation to express my opinion. But if I am the assistant to the Community, I may be able to say something personally to people but I don't have the right to interfere in the decision of the Community. I think that the people who were handling the Secular Order before me will be able, also, to testify, that one of the most frequent complaints received either in Provinces or generally are about a Spiritual Assistant who becomes dominators of Communities.

There is a Community that meets in a monastery of nuns. As the story goes, Mother Prioress handed a list of people to the President of the Secular Order telling them to enroll them as members of the Secular Order because they were their benefactors for that year. So they just enrolled them in the Secular Order; she just handed them the list, and they enrolled them in the Secular Order. They had something like 180 members on their list, and the majority of them were benefactors who had never seen the inside of the Secular Order meetings. There are other ways that people impose members, and this happens with assistants. My cousins, brothers-in-law, aunts, uncles, niece; "she is very holy, goes to Eucharistic Adoration every day. Your council has to decide this, etc., etc."

What are the responsibilities of the person who is the assistant to the Community? He does not interfere with the Council. The Council has the obligation to look after the good of the Community. The Council can only function if the Council is able to speak to each other. Anything that prevents a Councillor from being honest in expressing his/her opinion ,there is a question there as to whether or not the Council is a good Council. There is the necessity for confidentiality in the Council is number one. If I go to a Council meeting, whether I am a Councilor in my Province or the Provincial, and have to weigh what I am going to say because I am afraid somebody is going to repeat it, then the Holy Spirit is prevented from working in the Council. And if somebody comes to the Council and is afraid I am going to take it personally, that if they don't agree with me, therefore, they don't like me. Or if I am going to be hurt because somebody disagrees with me, there is something wrong with me. And because there is something wrong with me, in that sense I don't have the qualities necessary to be a good member of the Council.

In general, I will be going to India to visit all five provinces in India and sent ahead a letter to ask them to organize, as the first meeting in each Province, a meeting with the friars who are assistants to the Communities. It is a very difficult meeting to have because some have been Spiritual Assistants for twenty to thirty years and have done things in a certain way, and they are used to doing things that way, and they don't know the Constitutions and don't appreciate the change. Many times out of good will they say "I know they are going to try this, but I know it's not going to work because I remember fifteen years ago they tried it and it didn't work." So the Spiritual Assistant will step in and say "don't do that, you cannot do that, you have to do this." And this response from the Spiritual Assistant is out of good will. The unfortunate by-product of that response is that you (President and Councilors) don't learn that it doesn't work because you have to do what he says. Whereas, allowing the council to make the wrong decision and having to correct it is the idea in these Constitutions now that the Council has the authority and the Spiritual Assistant doesn't have the veto power, so the Council is responsible for its decisions good or bad. If you admit the wrong person to the Community to make Promises, it is your own fault. It's not the Spiritual Assistant's responsibility any more. You have to develop the courage to say "no" to people, which is not an easy thing to do. It has nothing to do with like or dislike; it has to do with "do they belong." Will they be good members of the Community. Now that is your decision to make in your Communities. The whole Council decides yes or no. And they have to inform the person; that's the hard part. (This goes back to the subject of meeting with Spiritual Assistants.) I like having meetings with assistants because it gives them the chance to ask questions apart from the Seculars because they don't always know if they are doing good or not. Nine times out of ten they are doing what they think is right. But they don't always understand that you, the Council, have to do it on your own.

Number 47 gives the A to Z of responsibilities, but number 46 it says that the primary responsibility of the Council is the formation of the Christian and Carmelite maturing of the members of the Community.

Election

Another important subject that I would like to discuss is the election in the Communities. We are human beings, we are Teresian Carmelites and Saint Teresa, of course, reminds us that it is stupid to think that we are angels as long as we have these bodies. And so we are going to be subject to anything that is human. Remembering that, elections are not popularity contests. If you are elected,, it is not because you are the most popular, hopefully it might be because you are the most capable. The most popular person in the Community may not be the most capable person in the Community for certain positions or certain jobs. And if you are not elected, it is not because you are not popular. I can give you an example of someone who was at the Congress in Mexico in the year 2000 who returned to her Province and was not elected President and left the Secular Order and left the Church, became a Presbyterian, as a matter of fact. We are capable of anything. Remember that. Election to a position in the Community is for the purpose of doing a service to the Community. No one is emperor or empress of the Secular Order. In the religious life, no one has a vocation to hierarchy. We are a Councillor or President, and then we go back to being a regular member.

The hierarchical structure belongs to the bishops and all other positions that go along with it. That's their structure. Our structure is completely on a rotation basis. You are and then you are not, and you might be again or you might not be again, but you are always a member. You are always a visible sign of the Church because you are a member, not because you are a President or a Councillor or the Formation Director. If your Community is only capable of having the same person as President or the same person as Formation Director, something is not working because part of the job of being a good Community is preparing people to be President and Formation Director. If you have a perpetual President or there is only one person who can do the formation and your council is always the same people (they just switch places), it's not working. The Holy Spirit is not able to breathe in circumstances being so confined. The Holy Spirit is able to work because we are flexible enough to do what God wants, all of us, together in the Community. One of the virtues of living in Community is "holy flexibility." We need this in the structures of our Communities. I have seen in some Communities a rigidity about a Community because it is the same people all the time. And the Community reflects those personalities instead of the one personality that we all owe allegiance; we have personalities taking the place of Jesus and that is because the Councils do not function as Councils. They function as positions and not in service but in control. Control is not service. Guidance, instruction, leadership—that is service, but not controlling.

It should be the responsibility of the three Councillors to form with the President and the Formation Director because the Director of Formation is part of the Council. One of the things that the Provincial Statutes are to determine is the procedure for election and the responsibilities of the three Councilors. The President's responsibilities are in number 51, and I want to underline one line of that, "...to foster a spirit of Christian and Carmelite affability being careful to avoid any demonstration of preference for some members over others." It sometimes happens that Presidents, especially if they do not have this mentality of the Constitutions, consult with other members of the Community who are not on the Council and they are the ones that decide, and the President brings their decision to the Council.

Fellowship

Concerning fellowship, I talked about Community and I talked about formation, information, and fellowship—the actual sharing/ wasting time together. If somebody has too many important things to do to spend time relaxing with you, they are not going to be good members of the Community. The Community prays together when you come to meetings, you receive instruction, and you discuss together important aspects of the Community, but there also has to be a fellowship part. This is taking a hint from Saint Teresa, when she was forming Saint John of the Cross to be a Discalced Carmelite in Chapter 17 (I think) in *The Book of Foundations,* talk about taking him to Valladolid and she said, although there were many things that he could teach me about prayer, the only thing I could really teach him was recreation, our style of community. So we take that hint that fellowship is actually part of formation or community. Recreation is a very Teresian term. We are going to recreation...we are going to waste time together. And for some people, it is a waste of time and they are not very good members of Community. If you don't know how to waste time together, you are not building a relationship. It's really not wasting time, it is using time to relax together. So the fellowship part is an integral part of your Community meetings. It's not just to get information, to do serious things, and it is also time to do what you do so well, chit chat. There are 3,500 Secular Order members in Korea, and they were in nine Communities. They didn't even know each other's names. So when I went there, I divided them into thirty-one Communities. They did not have the understanding of Community. They had the understanding of going, praying, listening to a lecture, and going home. They know a lot about Carmelite spirituality. but they need to develop into Communities. So there are two things: the leadership must be the Council that functions as a Council, and there must be fellowship in the Community because that is what gets over divisions, if you get to know everybody.

Secretary

The secretary is not a member of the Council. The Constitutions say that "The Secretary attends the Council meetings and records the minutes of the meeting without the right to vote." The Secretary is subject to the same confidentiality as the members of the Council. Confidentiality is also extended to the Treasurer, when he/she is at the meetings. Concerning minutes of the meeting, minutes should always be kept of the Council meetings. The next Council should know what has transpired before. The Secretary of the Council has the responsibility of keeping an up-to-date register of the Community, recording the elections, admissions, promises, and dismissals.

In general, if the Council begins to function with freedom and flexibility, then the Community begins to form itself as a Community.

Notes of Clarification

The Importance of Meetings

The Beatitudes point to the importance of meetings. The reason why meetings are so important is that you can't lead a spiritual life alone. You need to be in touch with, be supported by. and support others who are trying to do it too. We are incarnate. It's not just the Holy Spirit. We learn from each other; this is part of being community. It is for that reason, a little bit why, we have inched away from, some people have said maybe we have moved miles away from, the idea of isolate members, long-distance members from a distance, maybe in other ways, but they have to be associated with other people. It's too difficult to do this; it is too inhuman. It is not practical to set up a spiritual life and a solemn life all alone. If it is not practical, it's not Carmelite. Carmelite spirituality is supremely practical. It can be done and it can be practiced under certain conditions and in a certain way, and for this reason, community life, whether it is for us who live in Communities or for you who make Community, it is indispensable.

Does that make sense? So you have made the mistake that people make when they say, "Oh, I don't need to go to meetings anymore."

I am not talking about the sick. I am not talking about those who are reasonably, rationally excused or those who miss because their daughter is getting married or their husband is sick. I am talking about people who don't come. They don't come and they say, "Oh, I say my Office every day and I meditate every day."

There is more to it than that. It is not a training ground for individualists. Matter of fact, the one thing we lose is our individualism, not our individuality, of course, but our individualism. What grows in a person who makes this Promise, who tries to live these Beatitudes as an apostolate, is the need to have others, to understand what is the right thing to do. And the people who need to know this don't come anymore. So this is why we have to really relook at the way we do things. We cannot continue to make the mistake of forming individualists.

Again, there is always a question, Why is it that some people come to some Communities and turn away? Because they do not see in the Community the example of people who are living Carmelite spirituality. Especially if they come in and find groups, cliques, and divisions. They can find that in the office. It depends on how the Community is functioning as a Community. Is the Community functioning as a Community?

Negative Experiences

I am going to state a few one sentence principles that form the background of my comments.

> Principle 1: Negative people are not the majority, but they are the most vocal.
> Principle 2: Together we can be all things to all persons, but no individual can be all things to all persons.
> Principle 3: It is not necessary to be accepted by everybody in order to realize one's vocation.
> Principle 4: "Keep your eyes fixed on Christ Crucified and all will become small" applies in every circumstance of life, outside and inside the Order.
> Corollary of Principle # 4: Adversity, in God's hands, is an experience of grace.

Again, I think that negative people are few, but they are really loud in their negativity. Therefore, they are very noticeable. If your experience of a certain member of the Order is negative, I think if you examine well the circumstances, you might discover that the negativity is not just confined to the OCDS.

Sometimes the conflicts arise from the fact that some people interpret authority as control instead of leadership and empowerment.

Since you have the position of the Order, approved by the Holy See, expressed in your Constitutions and with that the support and encouragement of the General Superiors as Fathers of the Order, you really do not need anyone else's approval to be what you are called to be in Carmel. Yes, it is the responsibility of the friars to minister and empower you to live that call. Just remember that it is not necessary to have everybody's approval to do that.

The lives of our holy Parents, Saints Teresa of Jesus and John of the Cross, are the richest examples of dealing with adversity. Saint Teresa was called before the Inquisition twice. Saint John of the Cross spent nine months locked in a prison cell by Carmelite friars. Thank goodness they did not let their experiences of negativity embitter them!

Saint Teresa in the Interior Castle (VII, 4) writes "Poned los ojos en el Crucificado y todo se hará poco" (Keep your eyes on the Crucified One and everything will become small). I mean, we really did not join Carmel so that everybody would think well of us. I believe that the practical effect of obedience is to keep us focused on exactly where we get the direction of our lives. For me, the most efficient way of keeping my eyes fixed on the Lord is to cooperate in obedience with the legitimate superiors of the Order and the Church.

Saint John of the Cross has the famous saying, "adonde no hay amor, ponga amor, y sacará amor" (Where there is not love, put love, and you will draw love). He does not say "where there is no love, put love, and you will be loved." Guard against allowing any negative experience to make you negative.

The experience that our holy Parents had of adversity did not sour them but strengthened them in their identity and vocation.

For me, the bottom line is that your call and place in the Order is certified in the official documents of the Order that have been approved by the Church. That is the source of your identity. Anyone—friar, nun, or other secular—who has a view or an opinion that differs from what is found in those official sources is expressing a personal opinion, but should not at all be taken seriously.

Discernment and Formation.

I want to begin with a quote from *Christifideles Laici.* Number 63 on formation.

> "In the work of formation some convictions reveal themselves as particularly necessary and fruitful. First of all, there is the conviction that one cannot offer a true and effective formation to others if the individual has not taken on or developed a personal responsibility for formation: this, in fact, is essentially a "formation of self." In addition, there is the conviction that, at one and the same time, each of us is the goal and principle of formation: the more we are formed and the more we feel the need to pursue and deepen our formation. Still more will we be formed and be rendered capable of forming others. It is particularly important to know that the work of formation, while having intelligent recourse to the means and methods available from human science, is made more effective the more it is open to the action of God. Only the branch which does not fear being pruned by the heavenly vinedresser can bear much fruit for the individual and for others."

Do not fear being pruned. I have a whole program of formation, in parenthesis, because it is actually a whole program of information, all written out, which I have sort of gleaned from looking at formation programs from around the world: what can be done at different stages, but it's too early to give it out, because we are still not clear about the formation. If we just continue giving information to people as they go through formation classes, almost as if, you've seen the mistakes, and the mistakes come at voting time, and the Council. Well, she's so intelligent. She really loves Saint Thérèse; she knows everything about her or she really loves the Blessed Mother. She loves the scapular. Goodness sake, she wears it night and day, all the time, but you know she is a little disagreeable in Community, just a little disagreeable. You notice that every time this person comes into the meeting everybody shuts up. They don't want to set her off. When it comes time to vote, she really does know what she is talking about. It is not a matter of knowing what. It is a matter of knowing how. The "how" depends on a good "what." It is knowing how to live this life.

Why do we make people parts of our Community that we would never want to live with?

What does it do to the Community?

How does it affect the Community?

You've seen in the talk that I gave in New Orleans and you have seen it in other places where I have written where I talk about people who talk about Our Lady of Medjugorje hours and hours. It is obvious how that throws the Community off. So everybody can really see how if you really have wrong things, things that aren't Carmelite things, you can see why that person doesn't belong.

This is a far more fundamental question about people who can live these evangelical counsels, the spirit of evangelical counsels, and the Beatitudes. They have to have a certain human capacity for conversion. Human capacity, not spiritual conversion. Not aversion from sin. Not practicing virtues heroically, but a human capacity. There has to be an ability to be part of other people. That is your responsibility as Council members when it comes to vote. You can give a written test on Carmelite spirituality, on the Catechism of the Catholic Church, on all the documents that have ever been written, and a person can get A, A, A, B+, and still invite someone to become part of your Community who does not belong.

Number 36 in the Constitution talks about formation, and again the formation touches upon the Promise. The gradual introduction. It's gradual. It's step by step; nobody starts out at the finish point. Everybody starts out at the beginning point. The gradual introduction to the life of the Secular Order is structured in the following manner:

A sufficient period of contact with the Community for no less than six months. The purpose of this stage is that the applicant might become more familiar with the Community, with the people and the style of life and service to the Church proper to the Secular Order of the Teresian Carmel. This period also, you might want to say, the main reason, is to give the Community the opportunity to make an adequate discernment of the candidate.

What are you looking at? Not their intelligence, not their wisdom, not their knowledge, but their ability to relate to the people in the Community. This is not a private school of spirituality. This is an organization of Christ's faithful people, part of the Discalced Carmelite Order. It is a community of people. You are looking at the capacity of this person to be part of the Community.

After the initial period of contact, the Council of the Community may admit the applicant to a more serious period. Very important… the Council of the Community may, …may… may—this is not a factory that produces Secular Order members. It's the Council of the

Community may and may not. The Council of the Community may admit the applicant to a more serious period of formation that usually lasts for two years leading up to the First Promises. There is a purpose for the formation. It's to get the person in a position, mentally, emotionally, psychologically, intellectually, and spiritually to commit himself or herself to the Community.

Is that what guides the period of formation that is given in the first two years? Is this person going to incorporate herself or himself with these people? It's the Promise that does that. At the end of this stage, with the approval of the Council of the Community, the applicant may, may be invited to make the first promises to follow the evangelical counsels and to live in the spirit of the Beatitudes for a period of three years.

So, what is the formation for the promise? In the last three years of initial formation, there is a deeper study of prayer, the Scriptures, the Documents of the Church, the Saints of the Order, and formation in the apostolate of the Order. At the end of these three years, the applicant may be invited by the Council to make the Definitive Promise. The period of formation has for its purpose of making the Promise.

So you are looking at, who are these people who can form community with us? How does this person help me live my commitment to evaluate myself through Jesus, poor, chaste, obedient, in relationship to the world that suffers? How is this person going to help me do this? How can I help this person do this? The rest, the soul, that's the body of being a member of the order. It is that body that receives its energy, its power, its light, its guide from the spirituality of Saint Teresa and Saint John of the Cross, Saint Thérèse, Saint Edith Stein, Saint Teresa of the Andes, and Elizabeth of the Trinity. That's the energy, that's the light, that's how we know what we are doing, and that's how we do it as members of our Order. We have all of our lives to study that. One of the things I want to say is that in some programs of formation, there is too much in the initial stages and not enough body, not enough that weighs us down. Because if we put too much spirit in the formation, this is too much to handle. It becomes too heavy. Am I making sense? Do you follow what I am saying?

This is what the Church needs of us. If this is what the Church needs of us, then guess what, it is what God wants of us. You might have heard me. I don't know if I said it on the tape and in the talk in New Orleans, but all of us come to Carmel for our reasons. That all of us stay for God's reasons. Our reasons grow and change. As you know I was a diocesan priest before I became a Carmelite, in Philadelphia. I knew the nuns in Philadelphia, basically. This was before all sorts of divisions that exist now among the nuns; it was before then. When I went to Carmel, I really thought I was going to be contemplative. I know, I really thought I was going to live in a monastery some place and have a lot of time for reading. Now, here I am after twenty some years, I've put a hundred thousand miles in the air a year, and it's your fault. We don't stay in Carmel for our reasons. If we do stay in Carmel for our reasons, we never grow up, we never mature. We stay in Carmel for God's reasons.

Accompaniment

There is a word that is part of formation that wasn't always part of formation, and the word is "accompaniment." You accompany people in the process. Good formation depends on good information. It is not wrong to have the information, but it's wrong to settle for the information as the formation. It's not only necessary that we help people understand what they are supposed to do. It is necessary to understand how they do it. So there is an accompaniment; this is why you cannot have all the formation on one person.

Other people have to be involved in helping the formation program. If I am going to have classes where I'm giving information, fine, then give it all to me. I'll do it all, formation for the people in the first six months, formation for the people in the first two years, the people in the second period of three years, and the formation, I can give classes. Yeah, you can see how much I can talk. I can give classes all you want, but if you want me to actually accompany these people on the way, not being their spiritual director, not an invasion of their privacy, but there is a spiritual accompaniment that goes along. Those of you who do formation, you develop a relationship with the people in formation. They begin to talk with you about difficulties as they get to different points. So this is very true in some places.

It is very true in the Philippines. They have thirty-five to forty people in formation in their Communities, in initial formation. They divide them up and have four people for the first stage and four people for the second stage, they divide them up. It is a new approach of how to do the formation.

Before, maybe forty, fifty, or sixty years ago, the formation was on how to do mortification or penances. I think this was true of the Order, if you asked me when I first wanted to become a Discalced Carmelite, which was 1965, and somebody asked me why I wanted to become a Carmelite. Well, Carmelites don't eat meat, they sleep on boards, they do penances and mortification for the Church. They were ideals for me. That was how people defined who we were. They didn't define us as people who lived the spirituality of Saint Teresa and Saint John of the Cross. They defined us by the external things that we did. In many ways the formation, even of the tertiary, in those days in the Secular Order was the formation of how to do penances and what days you fasted on and what days you had feasts on. There was nothing wrong in the sense of they were not making a mistake.

They were doing what their times taught them to do, and they did it for the glory of God, and so that they could know God and become saints and die and go to heaven. It was all about doing the external things because you wanted to please God.

Information has changed now. We have different materials and different responsibilities now. So, part of the mistake we made in learning all this was we changed the information, but didn't change the formation. We are still learning how to do this. Now, we are learning. We have learned. We have to accompany people to do these things. It is not just sufficient to have a good class.

It is necessary to accompany these people in understanding the whole process of formation, gently. That is why all these periods of formation say no less than six months, two years, and three years. Rule of thumb, practical experience of the Church, the Church allows in law, if there is a set period of formation, you may add up to one half of that set period as an extension. If you say six months, and at the end of six months they are not sure, you are not sure, and it is more important for you to be sure, by the way; if you are not sure, you can add three more months. If they are for two years in that period of formation before First Promises, they're not sure, you're not sure, you can add up to one more year. At the end of three years, they're not sure, you're not sure, you can add up to a year and a half, in segments, three month segments, six month segments, because you want to make the right decision and you want them to make the right decision.

I was Provincial in my Province three times. I sent eleven people home in those three times. Sometimes I sent people home I liked and sometimes I accepted the profession of people I did not like because liking people has nothing to do with it. It is not whether you like them or not. The question is this. Are they whole? Do they have these requisites? If they are nice people, especially if it's your brother's, sister's, husband's, mother-in-law's daughter, that doesn't mean she/he has a vocation in Carmel to make profession.

This process, I think, becomes clearer with practice than it can be in theory. The question is, Is there a criterion or set of criteria that can be used in order to say no, if it is necessary to say no? My response is that it is something that becomes clearer as the practice goes of accompaniment, because you begin to see things. Pay attention to doubts. You are the formatter; you pay attention to doubts. You don't make them a cause for a persecution, and you don't whitewash them away. You pay attention until they go away. If they stay there, is something there? If they stay, and it's not the first time, you wait; you have six months for getting people familiar, maybe nine months if it is necessary.

If you are a formatter, we have so many means of communication available to us, through e-mail, through telephone, etc. You keep in touch with people along the way.

If you are a formatter, you want to keep in touch, because you want to accompany them. At times, you have nine months. They haven't made a promise yet, but they are beginning to have two, maybe three, years before they make the First Promise.

Always remember that we are not assembling Carmelites. We are forming Carmelites. I think it becomes apparent when a Formation Director says to the Council, "this person, I think, really has it." The Council has the opportunity to make observations objectively that might help make the Formation Director have an answer or might open the Formation Director's eyes to something that they are not seeing because they are too close. It works out with practice. The criterion is not set, because it's not objective, in the terms that it is not a test that you can pass or fail on. It is more under the influence of the Holy Spirit today.

Again, I am not defending anything of any course of action. I am defending the principle. The principle is that formation is not information. Formation is being accompanied in the process. You get someone joining Carmel, who has been formed personally in Our Lady of Medjugorje, who can take the information and twist it. If you don't have people who know what the information means, then it is not going to be the same information. You can take somebody who takes Saint John of the Cross and the *Ascent of Mt. Carmel* and so distorts the words of Saint John of the Cross, that you have people who are actually insulting the spirituality of Saint John of the Cross by living a kind of rigidity and mortification that is offensive to God. Using the words, they don't understand what is put to death in mortification. It is not you, it is not the self. There really has to be someone trained to give that information—to know what it means. This is the whole tradition of accompaniment in formation. You need to be an accompanier. I am against being satisfied with information.

Contemplation

Let me tell you the practical side of contemplation. I think the basic truth is that the more you look inward without abandoning the outward, the more integrated you would become with the outward. There are some people who look so inward that they disconnect from reality, the reality of life, the reality of family, the reality of work everyday, the reality of food to be eaten and prepared, the reality of schedules; they just disconnect. I think if you're connected to the outside, the more you become an inward person, (I am not saying this very professionally) but the more integrated you become as a whole person in connection with the world.

Well, let's clarify one thing. Many of us, when we use the word contemplative, especially as Carmelites, we have in mind, probably a lot of times, the example of Saint Thérèse of the Child Jesus and Saint Teresa. There are almost too many Carmelite nuns as saints, because we confuse contemplation with cloister and a cloistered style of life. Contemplative style of life is not a cloistered style of life. There are many people who have lived in cloisters, for many years who are still waiting to become contemplative, because contemplation, in Carmelite spirituality, is a gift of God. It is a quality of life as lived, gifted by God to be in relationship with him in that certain way that enhances that life, whether it is a nun in a cloister, a friar in a monastery, or a secular in a family, in work, in a parish of a secular priest. First thing is to clear up what do we mean by contemplation? We do not mean cloister, cloistered style of life. One of the readings I love is on the feast of Saint Francis de Sales, which is in Office of Readings, one of the examples he is using, if you're a mother of a family, you can't live like that of a Poor Clare nun. How much time it takes out of your day to do what you are supposed to do as laypeople. You can still be contemplative because it depends on God, number one. We don't practice contemplative prayer unless God gives us contemplation. There is no sense in feeling guilty about not being contemplative because it is up to God, not up to you. It is the quality of life that improves with this knowledge of God that comes through prayer, through meditation, through dedicating ourselves to some time for that contemplation.

The Rule and Constitutions

For eight hundred years there has been only one document in the tradition of Carmel that goes by the title "rule." That document is the Rule of Saint Albert. That Rule, together with the Rules of Saint Augustine, Saint Benedict, Saint Francis of Assisi, and Saint Dominic for the Western Church and Saint Basil for the Eastern Church, have been the official guides for religious families since the 1200s.

The Rule of Saint Albert is the one document that all Carmelites of both the OCarm. and OCD traditions have in common.

The OCD Friars have as official legislation the Rule of Saint Albert and the Constitutions approved by the Holy See that serve as a way to live the spirituality of the Rule for current times.

The OCD Nuns have as official legislation the Rule of Saint Albert and the Constitutions approved by the Holy See that serve as a way to live the spirituality of the Rule for current times.

The OCD Seculars have had a different development in history. They are not an independent branch of Carmel. As the Constitutions recognize in article 41, they are a dependent branch of the Order but with a distinct identity.

Before 1922 there were various regulations in different parts of Europe that guided the OCDS or Third-Order Carmelites according to countries. But remember that before 1922, the greatest majority of Catholics lived in Europe. From 1922 until 1974 (52 years), the OCDS had the first attempt at a common legislation that was called the Manual. This first attempt at a universal and common legislation was a result of the first Code of Canon Law, which became obligatory in 1918.

After the Council, the Order asked a committee of friars from different parts of the world to update the Manual. The result was the publication in 1974 of the document known as the Rule of Life. It was finally approved in 1979. Of course, the Manual ceased to be valid because the Church approved the Rule of Life.

The word "rule" used with this document was perhaps a misnomer because it may have caused confusion with the Rule of Saint Albert.

In any case, this legislation of 1979 was followed by a number of documents of the Church that necessitated a new approach. Those documents were the New Code of Canon Law (1983), *Christifideles*

Laici (1987), following the Synod on Laypersons in the Church; and *Vita Consecrata* (1997), following the Synod on Consecrated Life.

As a result of these documents, it was mandatory for the Order to look at the legislation of the Secular members and bring that legislation into line with the law and theology those documents expressed.

In the recognition of the place of Secular members within the family and Order of Carmel, it became understood that like the friars and nuns, it was time for the OCD Seculars to have as official legislation the Rule of Saint Albert and the Constitutions approved by the Holy See, which serve as a way to live the spirituality of the Rule for current times. At the OCDS International Congress in 2000, Mexico City, I made the following proposal:

"My first point for review is the use of the title 'Rule.' In the history of spirituality, the word Rule has been reserved for the most part to designate the original inspiration of the great spiritual traditions of religious orders in the Church. Generally the Rules are the Rule of Saint Benedict, the Rule of Saint Francis, the Rule of Saint Augustine, and the Rule of Saint Albert in the Western Church and the Rule of Saint Basil in the Eastern Church. These rules are approved by the Church. The entire family of Carmel has only one Rule, that of Saint Albert. By the phrase 'the entire family of Carmel,' I mean the friars, nuns affiliated and aggregated institutes, both religious and secular of both branches of the Order. In addition to the Rule of Saint Albert, and for the purposes of clarification and application, we all have Constitutions and/or Norms that accompany the Rule. The only group of Carmelites that has another 'rule' is the Secular Order. I would like to propose that the Secular Order join the rest of the Order in preserving the word Rule for the Rule of Saint Albert and, in place of the word Rule, designate the proper legislation of the Secular Order as Norms for Carmelite Seculars. I think that it would help us all to unite together under the one Rule."

The Constitutions, submitted to the Holy See, were approved finally and definitively in June 2003. The Constitutions replace entirely the Rule of Life as the Rule of Life replaced entirely the Manual. Anyone, priest or layperson, Carmelite or non-Carmelite, who says differently is entirely mistaken. Are these Constitutions infallible or irreplaceable? Absolutely not. It will be necessary to redo them again in another thirty, forty, or fifty years. Why is that? That is because the nature of Constitutions is to help the members (friars, nuns, and seculars) to live the spirituality of the Order in response to the needs of the world as the Church indicates and demands.

Order

I do want to make one little correction in the way you use the word "Order." The Order is not you and us. It's us. How does the Order make a commitment to you, when you make a commitment to the Order? Because they receive your commitment. They provide a place for you to meet. Mainly, your other people in your Community who are part of the Order, you're meeting with them. They're there every month for you. Not just you there every month for them. The Order makes a commitment. The commitment of the Order is to be there. This is your commitment to be there. The Order is not the friars, the Order is not the nuns, and the Order is not the seculars. The Order is the friars, the nuns and the seculars. Part of our mutual support is your mutual support to each other. If you lived over in one of those houses over there, and you wanted to become a Carmelite, you couldn't do it alone. You would have to find other Carmelites, and you found them. The Order made a commitment to you; it is there. At the end of six years, it is definitive. That is why it is called definitive; you are a member of the Order. Now it is your job to be there for others. The friars make a mistake all the time about the word Order; they think it is us, meaning friars. A little way of correcting that word, and understanding the word, how is the Order there, in the same way you are there for the people coming who are coming to your meeting now. The Order sets up a structure for us, for the nuns, and for you. We all become a part of that structure to be present.

Discalced Carmelites and The Members of the Ancient Observance (OCarm)

We both serve Christ; yes, but we both serve Christ differently. We are two different Orders. We have the same font, but it has produced different fruit. We have the same font in having the Rule of Saint Albert.

We have many things in common and we share many things in common, but not that which most identifies us in the way in which we are Carmelites. The one thing we do not have in common is the charism, that identifies, distinguishes us as Carmelites.

We as Discalced Carmelites, in many ways, look to Saint Teresa and Saint John of the Cross. The members of the Ancient Observance (OCarm) look to Saint Albert of Jerusalem, the Rule and the figure of Elijah. One of my professors in the courses I had in Spain said, "When I listen to Elijah, it is the voice of Teresa that tells me what he says." And so it is Teresa who very much identifies for us, what is in this charism that we have together in common. And she explains it in a way, different, than the explanation that the members of the Ancient Observance may understand things. Yes, we listen to Elijah. We listen to the Rule of Saint Albert. But it is the voice of our mother, Saint Teresa that tells us what it means.

Universal Church:

I sometimes say that Carmelites have the temptation to feel themselves dispensed from what the Church teaches because we are Carmelites. I got this a lot when I sent out original drafts about things and the importance of *Christifideles Laici* and all that *Christifideles Laici* says about the commitment necessary on the part of laypeople in the Church. It is like Saint John of the Cross says, that if you are contemplative, you don't have to do anything else. Well that depends on if God gave you contemplation, not whether you are making mental prayer, number one. Number two, it is a misunderstanding of what Saint John said, and they know nothing about Saint John of the Cross's life. So there is a temptation to think that because we are Carmelites, we do not have to do anything else that the Church says. In the formation programs, it is not necessary to cover everything about Saint Teresa or everything about Saint John of the Cross in the first few years. It is necessary to see if the person has the stamina and the commitment to make themselves available to this lifestyle in those initial years of formation. Then we have the whole rest of life. Ongoing formation is so important, because it gives us the opportunity for all of this to deepen.

Quotable Quotes

It is not any devotion to Our Lady that identifies a person called to the Secular Order. Mary is our model of prayer and meditation. This interest in learning to meditate or inclination to meditate is fundamental characteristic of any Secular Carmelite. It is perhaps the most basic.

****

Being a Carmelite is not a privilege. Being a Carmelite is a responsibility! Responsibility does not mean burden—it means the ability to respond to God who calls us and to respond to the world that need to know God.

****

Carmel has a mission. Carmel's mission is that we know God so that God may be known.

****

There are a lot of other people who are part of the Carmelite family who are not part of the Order. There are a lot of people who know a lot of things about Carmelite spirituality and really are experts but are not members of the Order. What makes you a member of the Secular Order is that you have made the Promise.

Sometimes the conflicts arise from the fact that some people interpret authority as control instead of leadership and empowerment.

****

Election to a position in the Community is for the purpose of doing a service to the community…. Our structure is completely on a rotation basis. You are and then you are not, and you might be again or you might not be again, but you are always a member. You are always a visible sign of the Church because you are a member, not because you are President or a Council or the Formation Director.

****

The justice that exists in the Bible is not the justice that you and I say, as Americans, when we say justice is going to be done. We mean justice as punishment. We mean justice as revenge. This is not at all evangelical. This is not at all scriptural…. Justice is to look out for the poor; justice is to make sure people eat; justice is to make sure people are clothed. Justice is to make sure people have what they need to be human and to live humanly. Justice is to forgive.

Notes

Notes

Notes

Notes

Notes

Notes